STUDENT'S BOOK & WORKBOOK

Carla Maurício Vianna
Charis Hannah
Gisele Aga
Henrick Oprea
João Gabriel Schenferd
Megha Ramesh

Head of Product - Pearson Brasil	Juliano de Melo Costa
Product Manager - Pearson Brasil	Marjorie Robles
Product Coordinator - ELT	Mônica Bicalho
Authors	Carla Maurício Vianna Gisele Aga Henrick Oprea
Teacher's Guide	Carla Maurício Vianna Gisele Aga
Workbook	Charis Hannah Gisele Aga Megha Ramesh João Gabriel Schenferd
Editor - ELT	Gisele Aga Renata S. C. Victor
Editor (Teacher's Book)	Simara H. Dal'Alba (Allya Assessoria Linguística)
Editorial Assistant - ELT	Simara H. Dal'Alba (Allya Assessoria Linguística)
Proofreader (English)	Silva Serviços de Educação
Proofreader (Portuguese)	Fernanda R. Braga Simon
Copyeditor	Maria Estela Alcântara
Pedagogical Reviewer	Najin Lima
Quality Control	Viviane Kirmeliene
Art and Design Coordinator	Rafael Lino
Art Editor - ELT	Emily Andrade
Acquisitions and permissions Manager	Maiti Salla
Acquisitions and permissions team	Cristiane Gameiro Heraldo Colon Maricy Queiroz Sandra Sebastião Shirlei Sebastião
Graphic design	Mirella Della Maggiore Armentano MRS Consultoria Editorial
Graphic design (cover)	Mirella Della Maggiore Armentano MRS Consultoria Editorial
Media Development	Estação Gráfica
Audio	Maximal Studio
Audiovisual Editor	Tatiane Almeida
Audiovisual	Desenrolados

The publisher would like to thank the following for their kind permission to reproduce their photographs:

123RF: p. 73. **ACPE**: p. 57. **Baldo**: p. 41. **Bridgeman**: p. 47. **Calvin & Hobbes**: p. 41, 116. **Cartoonstock**: p. 23. **Cathy Guisewite**: p. 40, 80. **Drable, Kevin Fagan**: p. 40. **Dreamstime**: p. 20, 56. **Food and Agriculture Organization of United Nations (FAO)**: p. 24. **Harvard T.H. Chan - School of Public Health**: p. 20 (Healthy eating plate). **iStock**: capa, p. 12, 13, 15, 18, 25, 27, 28, 32, 35, 53, 55, 56 (skateboarding), 61, 63, 71, 73, 106, 107, 108, 120. **Jump Start**: p. 40, 44. **King Features Syndication**: p. 116. **Met Museum**: p. 50. **Ministério da Saúde**: p. 109. **Paws**: p. 69. **Penguin Modern Classics**: p. 72, 78. **Shutterstock**: p. 9, 11, 17, 45, 46, 47, 59. **Stuart Carlson**: p. 80. **The Diana Award**: p.42. **Wonder Plugin**: p. 60

Every effort has been made to trace the copyright holders and we apologize in advance for any unintentional omissions. We would be pleased to insert the appropriate acknowledgement in any subsequent edition of this publication.

Dados Internacionais de Catalogação na Publicação (CIP)
(Câmara Brasileira do Livro, SP, Brasil)

Expand 1: Student's Book / Carla Maurício Vianna... [et al.]. -- São Paulo: Pearson Education do Brasil, 2019.

Outros autores: Charis Hannah, Gisele Aga, Henrick Oprea, João Gabriel Schenferd, Megha Ramesh.

ISBN 978-65-5011-028-4

1. Inglês (Ensino Médio) I. Vianna, Carla Maurício. II. Hannah, Charis. III. Aga, Gisele. IV. Oprea, Henrick. V. Schenferd, João Gabriel. VI. Ramesh, Megha.

19-25472   CDD-420.7

Índices para catálogo sistemático:
1. Inglês: Ensino Médio 420.7
Maria Alice Ferreira - Bibliotecária - CRB-8/7964

ISBN 978-65-50110-28-4 (Student's Book & Workbook)
ISBN 978-65-50110-29-1 (Teacher's Book)

2019

EXPAND 1

❯ **Unit 1**	9
❯ **Unit 2**	17
❯ Review 1	25
❯ **Unit 3**	27
❯ **Unit 4**	35
❯ Review 2	43
❯ **Unit 5**	45
❯ **Unit 6**	53
❯ Review 3	61
❯ **Unit 7**	63
❯ **Unit 8**	71
❯ Review 4	79
Grammar Overview	81
Language Reference	85
Reading Strategies	93
Irregular Verbs	94
Common Mistakes	96
False Friends	97
Glossary	98
Workbook	103
Audio Scripts	136

CONTENTS

	READING	VOCABULARY IN USE	LANGUAGE IN USE 1	EXPAND YOUR READING	LANGUAGE IN USE 2	LISTENING COMPREHENSION
UNIT 1 Migration Trends — page 9	Article: What are the pull and push factors of migration?	Suffixes used to form adjectives	Simple present	Ad campaigns about immigration	Imperative form	Opinions about immigration
UNIT 2 "The First Wealth is Health" — page 17	Quiz: Healthy eating	Food items and nutrition	Simple present: interrogative form and frequency adverbs	Tips for making healthy eating decisions	Subject and object pronouns	Dietary guidelines around the world

Review 1 (Units 1-2) — Page 25

	READING	VOCABULARY IN USE	LANGUAGE IN USE 1	EXPAND YOUR READING	LANGUAGE IN USE 2	LISTENING COMPREHENSION
UNIT 3 Your Digital Self — page 27	Social media posts	False friends	Present simple vs. present continuous	Pros and cons of social media	Possessive adjectives	Social media extracts
UNIT 4 Establishing and Keeping Relationships — page 35	Magazine article: How the teen brain transforms relationships	Phrasal verbs related to relationships	Simple past	Comic strips about different kinds of relationship	Modal verbs: *can* and *should*	Bullying advice: an anti-bullying campaign

Review 2 (Units 3-4) — Page 43

Grammar Review — page 81

Language Reference — page 85

Reading Strategies — page 93

Irregular Verbs — page 94

	READING	VOCABULARY IN USE	LANGUAGE IN USE 1	EXPAND YOUR READING	LANGUAGE IN USE 2	LISTENING COMPREHENSION
UNIT 5 Art: The Language of Emotions » page 45	Article: The most relevant art today is taking place outside the art world	Prefixes	Plural of nouns	Museum artifact descriptions	Order of adjectives	An artist talking about his work
UNIT 6 Sport is No Longer Just Sport » page 53	Seminar series calendar: Power and politics of sports	Suffixes used to form nouns	Comparative adjectives	News report about the Olympic Games Tokyo 2020	Superlative adjectives	A talk about millennials' impact on the sports industry

Review 3 (Units 5-6)
» page 61

	READING	VOCABULARY IN USE	LANGUAGE IN USE 1	EXPAND YOUR READING	LANGUAGE IN USE 2	LISTENING COMPREHENSION
UNIT 7 Globish: Fad or Fact? » page 63	Newspaper article: So, what's this Globish revolution?	Idioms	The 's for possession: the genitive case	Book summary: *The Future of English?*	Possessive pronouns	A talk about English being a global language
UNIT 8 Hit the Road » page 71	Book excerpt: *The Great Railway Bazaar*	Packing for a trip and means of transportation	*Used to*	Tips on how to travel with only a carry-on bag	Modal verb: *must*	An interview about traveling on a radio show

Review 4 (Units 7-8)
» page 79

Common Mistakes
» page 96

False Friends
» page 97

Glossary
» page 98

Workbook
» page 103

Audio Scripts
» page 136

PRESENTATION

STUDENT'S BOOK

Welcome to the *Expand* collection! *Expand* prepares students for the English part of Brazilian exams ENEM and vestibular, which are aimed at testing students' ability to read a wide variety of authentic texts of different genres. *Expand* provides students with listening, speaking, and writing activities that help them to develop their overall knowledge of the language. Each thematic unit contains two reading sections that introduce grammar and vocabulary topics, as well as listening comprehension activities that give students contact with oral text genres.

OPENING PAGE

Each unit starts with an opening page containing:

IN THIS UNIT YOU WILL…

This shows the main objectives for the unit.

LEAD OFF

This section presents three to four questions for content contextualization.

> ▶ **IN THIS UNIT YOU WILL…**
> - talk about migration and its causes and results;
> - use the simple present to describe facts and routines;
> - use the imperative form to make requests and provide directions.

- What documents can you see in the picture?
- What does the word *immigration* mean to you?
- Why do people migrate?

READING PAGES

This two-page section contains the first reading text and activities of the unit. It develops reading strategies and is subdivided into the following stages:

BEFORE READING

This section contains one or two activities that help students to prepare for the text topic, which is presented in the section WHILE READING.

READING

BEFORE READING — *Bridging and relating to the topic*

1. Not everything you read about nutrition is true. Read the statements and guess the ones that are not true. Then, check with your teacher.

WHILE READING

In this section students read a text and answer a question related to it. Texts are a variety of different genres and aimed at developing several reading strategies.

WHILE READING

Read part of an article about the Globish revolution. According to the writer, is it easier or harder to communicate with business people using Globish? — *Scanning*

So, what's this Globish revolution?

I say tomato… you say red, round fruit. Increasingly, people across the world use some sort of English, but it is not the Queen's. Robert McCrum, Observer Literary Editor, reports on why Globish - English-lite - is becoming the universal language of the boardroom…

AFTER READING

This section has comprehension activities to help develop different after-reading strategies related to reading comprehension. These strategies are presented next to the instruction for each reading activity.

VOCABULARY PAGES

This stage develops students' vocabulary through activities containing vocabulary from the text and related to the topic of the unit.

EXPAND YOUR VOCABULARY

This section contains one to three activities related to the vocabulary presented in the text. It also prompts students to engage in conversational topics based on the text they have read.

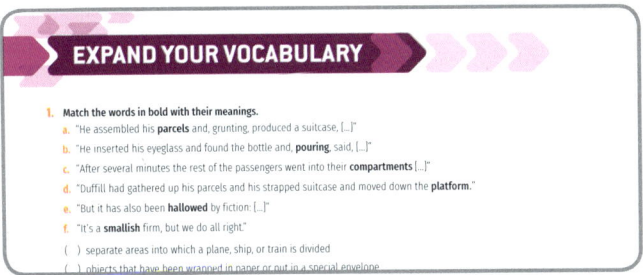

VOCABULARY IN USE

Here students are presented with an example of target vocabulary taken from the main reading text and do activities to develop their vocabulary knowledge.

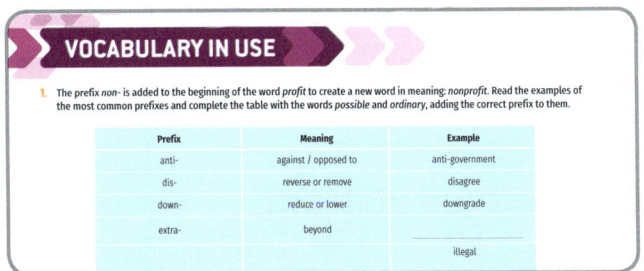

LANGUAGE IN USE 1

This page presents the first grammar topic of the unit. It contains examples from the text and activities that develop students' grammar knowledge in the target language.

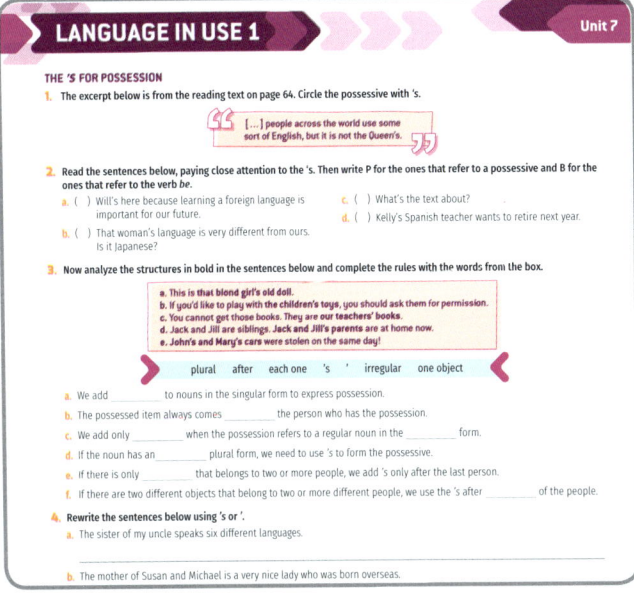

EXPAND YOUR READING

This section contains another text for students to work on both the text genre and comprehension.

PRESENTATION

LANGUAGE IN USE 2

This page presents the second grammar topic of the unit. It contains examples from the text in *Expand your reading* and activities that develop students' grammar knowledge in the target language.

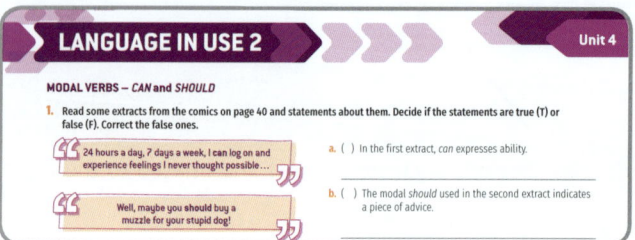

WORKBOOK

Each unit has four pages of reading, vocabulary, and grammar activities. It also has an ENEM or vestibular question in the section AN EYE ON ENEM / VESTIBULAR.

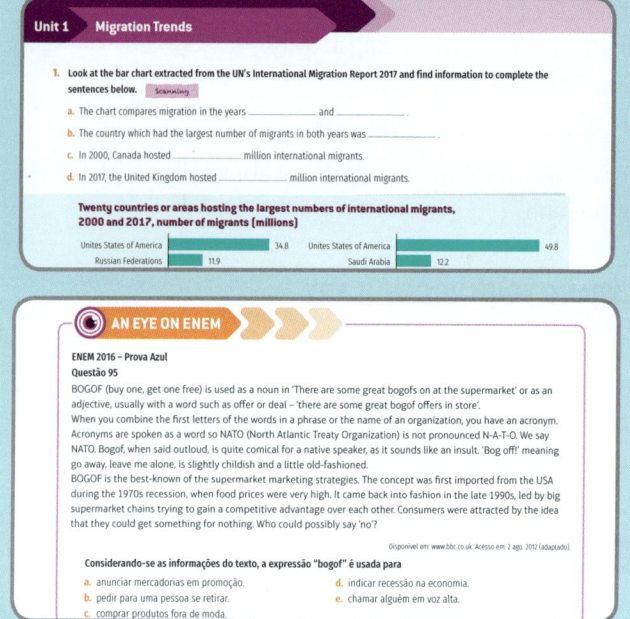

LISTENING COMPREHENSION

This section contains listening activities with authentic texts aimed at developing students' listening skills.

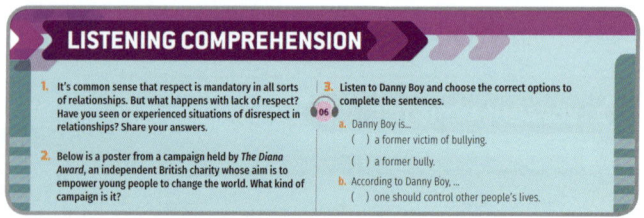

EXPAND YOUR HORIZONS

In this end-of-unit section, students are presented with three statements that allow them to discuss the topic in the listening comprehension section and think critically about it while using the target language.

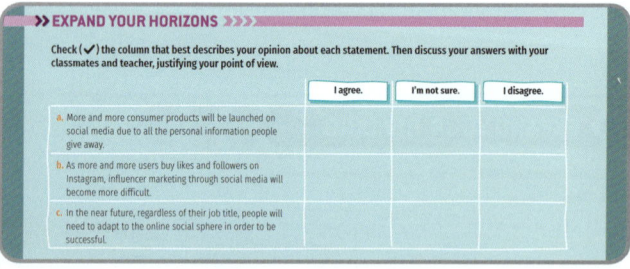

DIGITAL COMPONENTS

Video lessons for all *Language in Use* and *Vocabulary in Use* sections and for exam practice.

Mock test generator with major Brazilian *Vestibular* and ENEM questions to prepare students for these exams.

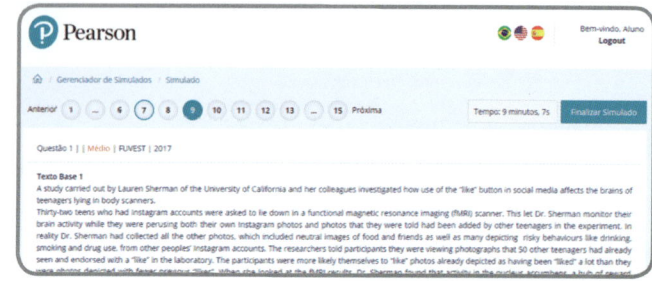

REVIEW

Every two units there is a two-page section for students to review and practice the language they have learned so far.

UNIT 1

Migration Trends

▶ IN THIS UNIT YOU WILL…

- talk about migration and its causes and results;
- use the simple present to describe facts and routines;
- learn how to form adjectives using suffixes;
- use the imperative form to make requests and provide directions.

- What documents can you see in the picture?
- What does the word *immigration* mean to you?
- Why do people migrate?

READING

>> BEFORE READING — Relating to the topic

There are several reasons why people migrate. Number the reasons from 1 (the most common) to 4 (the least common) in your opinion.

_____ environmental _____ economic _____ cultural _____ socio-political

> **migrate** [intransitive + *from/to*] if people migrate, they go to live in another area or country, especially in order to find work
>
> Extracted from www.ldoceonline.com/dictionary/migrate. Accessed on May 4, 2018.

>> WHILE READING — Skimming

Skim the text to find out its main objective. Then check (✓).

a. (   ) To describe the writer's own experiences.
b. (   ) To inform the reader about why people migrate.

---

http://eschooltoday.com/migration/the-pull-and-push-factors-of-migration.html

What are the Pull and Push Factors of Migration?

People migrate for a number of reasons. These reasons may fall under these four areas: *Environmental, Economic, Cultural,* and *Socio-political*. Within these areas, the reasons may also be '*push*' or '*pull*' factors.

Push Factors

Push factors are those that force the individuals to move voluntarily, and in many cases, they are forced because they risk something if they stay. Push factors may include *conflict, drought, famine,* or extreme religious activity.

Poor economic activity and lack of job opportunities are also strong push factors for migration. Other strong push factors include race, discriminating cultures, political *intolerance,* and *persecution* of people who question the **status quo**.

Pull Factors

Pull factors are those in the destination country that attract the individual or group to leave their home. Those factors are known as "place utility", which is the **desirability** of a place that attracts people. Better economic opportunities, more jobs, and the promise of a better life often pull people into new locations.

Sometimes individuals have ideas and perceptions about places that are not necessarily correct, but are strong pull factors for them. As people grow older and **retire**, many look for places with warm weather and peaceful and comfortable locations to spend their retirement after a lifetime of hard work and savings. Such ideal places are pull factors too.

Very often, people consider and prefer different opportunities closer to their location than similar opportunities farther away. In the same vein, people often like to move to places with better cultural, political, climatic, and general terrain located closer to them. It is rare to find people who move very long distances to **settle** in places that they have little **knowledge** of.

Adapted from http://eschooltoday.com/migration/the-pull-and-push-factors-of-migration.html. Accessed on June 25, 2018.

Unit 1

»AFTER READING

1. Label the pictures according to the dictionary entries below. Can you exchange the labels of the pictures? Why (not)? *Understanding main ideas*

> **immigrant**
> someone who enters another country to live there permanently
>
> **refugee**
> someone who has been forced to leave their country, especially during a war, or for political or religious reasons
>
> *Extracted from www.ldoceonline.com/dictionary/refugee. Accessed on June 26, 2018.*

a.

b.

2. Underline the incorrect information in each statement. *Understanding details*

a. Poor economic activity and a great number of job opportunities are also strong push factors for migration.

b. Push factors do not include conflict, drought, famine, or extreme religious activity.

c. Push factors are those in the destination country that attract the individual or group to leave their home.

d. As people grow older and retire, some look for places with warm weather.

3. Rewrite the statements from activity 2 with the correct information.

a. _____

b. _____

c. _____

d. _____

EXPAND YOUR VOCABULARY

1. Find the words in *italics* in the reading. Then match each word with its meaning.

( ) conflict   a. unwillingness to accept ways of thinking and behaving that are different from your own

( ) drought   b. a long period of time when there is little or no rain

( ) famine   c. a state of disagreement or argument between people, groups, countries, etc.

( ) intolerance   d. a situation in which a large number of people have little or no food for a long time and many people die

( ) persecution   e. cruel or unfair treatment of someone over a period of time, especially because of their religious or political beliefs

2. What about your country or the area where you live? Does it have any of the issues mentioned above? Use some of the vocabulary from activity 1 to write a statement describing a similar issue where you live.

_____

11

VOCABULARY IN USE

1. The suffix -al is used to form adjectives from nouns, with the meaning "relating to". The word *cultural* in the text means "relating to a particular society and its way of life". Go back to the text on page 10 and find other adjectives formed using the suffix -al.

   _____

2. Use the following adjectives to complete the sentences.

   > environmental   international   musical   political   presidential <

   a. They are a very _____ family.
   b. Ocean pollution is a serious _____ issue.
   c. This is an event organized by _____ activists.
   d. A large crowd was in front of the _____ palace.
   e. Immigration is an important _____ issue.

3. Use the suffixes in the columns to create new words from the words in the box.

   > access   adventure   artist   attract   danger   economy
   > harm   help   hope   invent   sleeve   understand <

-able / -ible	-ful	-ic / -ical	-ive	-less	-ous

4. Complete the sentences below with some adjectives from the table in activity 3.

   a. My brother is highly _____. He loves to create new things.

   b. It's terribly hot here in the summer, so wear _____ shirts.

   c. She is such an _____ girl that she is always looking for a new place to visit.

   d. Susan is such a nice and _____ girl. She always offers help when needed.

   e. The hotel is only _____ by boat as it is located on a island.

   f. I love to watch the _____ in the synchronized swimming event in the Olympics.

5. Work with a partner. Describe one person and one thing in you classroom using adjectives with suffixes.

   _____

   _____

LANGUAGE IN USE 1

Unit 1

SIMPLE PRESENT

1. Read these excerpts from the text on page 10. Focus on the underlined words. Then decide if the statements are true (T) or false (F).

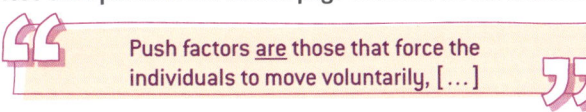
"Push factors are those that force the individuals to move voluntarily, […]"

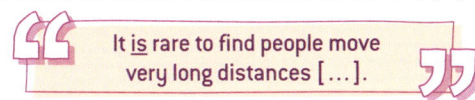
"It is rare to find people move very long distances […]."

a. ( ) Based on the sentences we can say that *be* is a stative verb, that is, there is no action described.

b. ( ) Both sentences have the verb *be* as the main verb.

c. ( ) The verb *be* in the simple present has the same form for all subjects.

2. Now analyze the structures in bold in the excerpts below and check (✓) the option that corresponds to what they express.

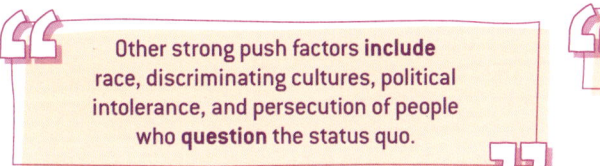
"Other strong push factors **include** race, discriminating cultures, political intolerance, and persecution of people who **question** the status quo."

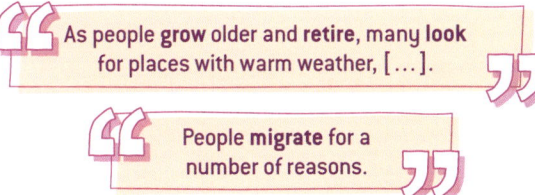
"As people **grow** older and **retire**, many **look** for places with warm weather, […]."

"People **migrate** for a number of reasons."

a. ( ) Something that is true in the present or something that happens again and again in the present.

b. ( ) Something that is happening at the moment of speaking.

c. ( ) Something which we think is temporary.

3. Complete the texts with the appropriate form of the verbs in parentheses.

a. Migration _____ (occur / occurs) primarily between countries that _____ (is / are) located within the same world region. In 2017, the majority of the international migrants originating from Europe (67%), Asia (60%), Oceania (60%) and Africa (53%) _____ (reside / resides) in a country located in their region of birth.
In contrast, international migrants from Latin America and the Caribbean (84%) and Northern America (72%) reside primarily outside their region of birth.

Extracted from www.un.org/en/development/desa/population/migration/publications/ migrationreport/docs/MigrationReport2017_Highlights.pdf. Accessed on March 6, 2018.

b. Globally, the twenty largest countries or areas of origin _____ (account / accounts) for almost half (49%) of all international migrants, while one-third (34%) of all international migrants _____ (originate / originates) in only ten countries. India _____ (is / are) now the country with the largest number of people living outside the country's borders ("diaspora"), followed by Mexico, the Russian Federation, and China.

Adapted from www.un.org/en/development/desa/population/migration/ publications/migrationreport/docs/MigrationReport2017_Highlights.pdf. Accessed on March 6, 2018.

4. Use the verbs from the box to complete the extract below.

> arrive   marks   sit   wait

[…] The broken line snakes back 8 miles (13 km) to the border crossing at Paraguachon, where more than a hundred Venezuelans _____ in the heat outside the migration office.

Money changers _____ at tables stacked with wads of Venezuelan currency, made nearly worthless by hyperinflation under President Nicolas Maduro's socialist government.

The remote outpost on the arid La Guajira peninsula on Colombian's Caribbean coast _____ a frontline in Latin America's worst humanitarian crisis.

The Venezuelans _____ hungry, thirsty, and tired, often unsure where they will spend the night, but relieved to have escaped the calamitous situation in their homeland. […]

Adapted from www.reuters.com/article/us-colombia-venezuela-migrants/ migrate-or-die-venezuelans-flood-into-colombia-despite-crackdown-idUSKCN1GA1K9. Accessed on March 7, 2018.

EXPAND YOUR READING

1. Read these ad campaigns and complete the sentences with the corresponding letters.

   a. Ads _____, _____, and _____ are for immigration and ad _____ is against immigration.
   b. Ad _____ gives a warning for people not to do something.

Extracted from us.iasservices.org.uk/I-Am-An-Immigrant-Poster-Campaign-Highlights-Positives-Of-Immigration. Accessed on May 6, 2018.

Extracted from weeklydialog.wordpress.com/2013/01/31/britain-0-vs-romania-1-ad-campaign-to-put-off-potential-immigrants/. Accessed on March 7, 2018.

Extracted from www.jigsaw-online.com/category/new/shop-the-campaign. Accessed on May 6, 2018.

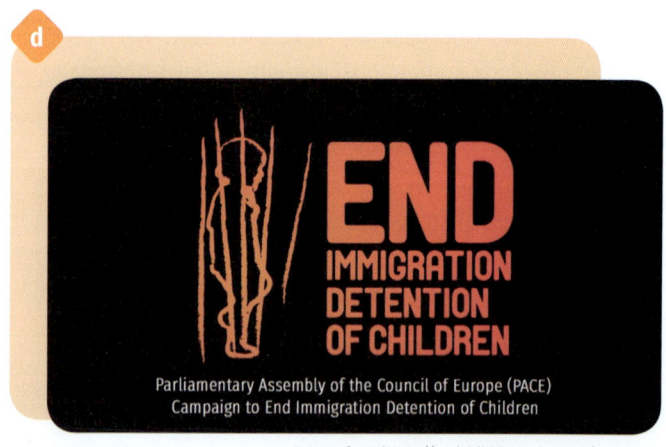

Extract from https://endchilddetention.org/. Acessed on November 11, 2018.

2. Underline the correct option to complete the statements according to the ad campaigns you've just read.

   a. The objective of the ads is to **encourage product sales** / **advertise an idea**.
   b. **All of them** / **Some of them** use appealing images.
   c. They **provoke** / **don't provoke** negative and positive social judgement.

LANGUAGE IN USE 2

Unit 1

IMPERATIVE FORM

1. Go back to the ads on the previous page and look at the verb *end*. It is in the affirmative imperative form. Why is this form of the verb used? Check (✓) the correct alternative.
   a. ( ) To give the target audience an instruction, a suggestion, or an order.
   b. ( ) To describe what is going on in each ad.

2. *Don't come* is in the negative imperative form. To form the negative imperative we use…

   _____ ➕ the infinitive form of the verb without *to*

3. Complete the instructions with the correct imperative form of the verbs in the box. Then match the instructions with the signs.

   > turn off   take   go   turn   eat   swim   drink <

   a. _____ or _____ here.
   b. _____ right.
   c. _____ in the lake.
   d. _____ straight ahead.
   e. _____ pictures.
   f. _____ your cell phone.

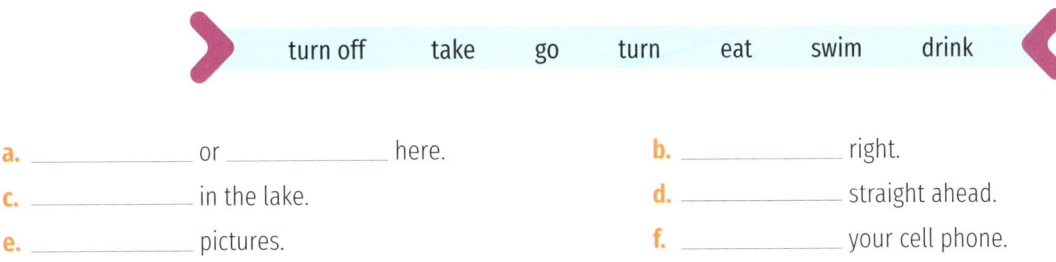

LISTENING COMPREHENSION

1. **Why are some people against immigration? Talk to a classmate and list some reasons. Then exchange ideas with your classmates and teacher.**

   _____
   _____
   _____

2. **You are going to listen to some people talking about immigration. Label the excerpts a-e in the order you hear them.**

   🎧 02

   ( ) "Make us feel safe. We need to feel safe in this country. I think there's a great divide between the races."

   Extracted from www.usatoday.com/pages/interactives/trump-nation/#/?_k=wi8jwl
   Accessed on May 7, 2018.

   ( ) "I don't feel as though I have to validate my existence as a citizen of the United States or of the world by my accomplishments but all of my accomplishments are driven by my family and where we're from."

   Extracted from https://edition.cnn.com/videos/us/2018/01/12/
   Accessed on March 7, 2018.

   ( ) "I believe that he will make America great again and that means a return of jobs. So, in that manner maybe I will find employment."

   Extracted from www.usatoday.com/pages/interactives/trump-nation/#/?_k=wi8jwl
   Accessed on May 7, 2018.

   ( ) "When Mexico sends its people, they're not sending the best. They're sending people that have lots of problems and they're bringing those problems."

   Extracted from www.cbsnews.com/pictures/wild-donald-trump-quotes/9.
   Accessed on May 6, 2018.

   ( ) "We have learned to love this country, Mr. President. This country does not belong to you only, but it belongs to all of us."

   Extracted from https://edition.cnn.com/videos/us/2018/01/12/
   Accessed on March 7, 2018.

   ( ) "We are able to move to these foreign countries where we don't know the language, we don't know the lifestyle, and adapt fairly quickly."

   Extracted from https://edition.cnn.com/videos/us/2018/01/12/
   Accessed on March 7, 2018.

3. **Which testimonials do you think are said by immigrants? Why?**

» EXPAND YOUR HORIZONS »»»

Check (✓) the column that best describes your opinion about each statement. Then discuss your answers with your classmates and teacher, justifying your point of view.

	I agree.	I'm not sure.	I disagree.
a. Racism and xenophobia are feelings that local people may develop against immigrants.			
b. Immigration is a characteristic of our globalized world that has both positive and negative effects on the economy of a country.			
c. Cosmopolitan cities are multicultural because of their large immigrant population.			

STUDY THIS

xenophobia

strong fear or dislike of people from other countries

Extracted from www.ldoceonline.com/dictionary/xenophobia. Accessed on July 17, 2018.

UNIT 2
"The First Wealth is Health"
R. Emerson

▶ IN THIS UNIT YOU WILL...

- talk about nutritional information in Brazil and around the world;
- discuss healthy eating habits;
- use the simple present to ask and answer questions;
- use adverbs of frequency;
- learn how to use subject and object pronouns.

LEAD OFF

- What can you see in the picture?
- How does the picture relate to your eating habits?
- Read the title of the unit: do you agree with the quote by the American poet Ralph Waldo Emerson?
- What do you consider healthy eating?

READING

>> BEFORE READING   *Bridging and relating to the topic*

1. Not everything you read about nutrition is true. Read the statements and guess the ones that are <u>not</u> true. Then check with your teacher.
   a. (   ) Lunch is the most important meal of the day.
   b. (   ) People with diabetes don't need to give up sweets.
   c. (   ) Carbohydrates aren't part of a healthy diet.
   d. (   ) Milk is one of the best and cheapest calcium sources.
   e. (   ) Egg yolks are unhealthy.

2. Work in small groups. Discuss the statements from activity 1. Relate the myths or facts to your reality at home and at school.

>> WHILE READING

1. Look at the text's layout and title. Then read the statements below and underline the one that best summarizes it.   *Skimming*
   a. The text persuades readers to buy a product.
   b. The text invites readers to join an event.
   c. The text measures readers' knowledge about a topic.

2. Take the Fruit Quiz below and test your knowledge.

---

https://www.choosemyplate.gov/quiz

Quiz Time!

QUESTION 1
Which of these nutrients can you get from eating whole fruit that is not usually found in juice?
(   ) Vitamins   (   ) Minerals   (   ) Fiber   (   ) Sugar

QUESTION 2
Potassium is a nutrient that many Americans don't get enough of. Which of the following is a good fruit source of this mineral known to help regulate **blood pressure**?
(   ) **Dried apricots**   (   ) Orange juice
(   ) Bananas   (   ) All of the above

QUESTION 3
Which fruit is this?
(   ) **Cantaloupe**   (   ) **Star fruit**
(   ) Papaya   (   ) **Moon fruit**
(   ) Mango

QUESTION 4
Eating a diet rich in fruits and vegetables as part of an overall healthy diet may protect against certain types of cancer.
(   ) True   (   ) False

QUESTION 5
Which of the following counts as part of the Fruit Group?
(   ) **Canned** peaches   (   ) Fresh strawberries
(   ) Dried apricots   (   ) All of the above
(   ) 100% orange juice

QUESTION 6
Fiber found in fruit is associated with which of the following health **outcomes**?
(   ) **Strengthening** bones
(   ) Maintaining proper **bowel** function
(   ) Building muscle
(   ) Making new blood cells

QUESTION 7
Fruits are sources of which of the following?
(   ) Folate   (   ) Vitamin D   (   ) Calcium   (   ) Protein

QUESTION 8
Which of these foods is actually a fruit in plant biology?
(   ) Onion   (   ) **Mushrooms**
(   ) Pepper   (   ) All of the above

QUESTION 9
Which of these foods is a **source** of vitamin C?
(   ) Pineapples   (   ) Oranges
(   ) Strawberries   (   ) All of the above

QUESTION 10
What do fruits have that make them sweet?
(   ) Vitamin C   (   ) Protein
(   ) Fiber   (   ) **Pleasing** or **agreeable** personalities
(   ) Fructose

Extracted from www.choosemyplate.gov/quiz. Accessed on May 11, 2018.

» AFTER READING

1. Check the answers to the quiz. Compare your results to a classmate's. *Understanding main ideas*

QUESTION 1

Correct Answer: Fiber

Fiber is found in the pulp of the fruit. When juice is made, the pulp is usually removed. Unfortunately, the fiber goes with it.

QUESTION 2

Correct Answer: All of the above

Potassium is a nutrient found in a wide variety of foods – from fruits to some beans (white beans, soy beans), vegetables (spinach, potatoes), fish (halibut, tuna), and low-fat yogurt and milk, too.

QUESTION 3

Correct Answer: Mango

Mango is a fruit that can be eaten raw or added to recipes, such as a stir fry, for added sweetness.

QUESTION 4

Correct Answer: True

As a part of an overall healthy diet, eating a diet rich in fruits and vegetables may reduce risk for heart disease, protect against certain types of cancer, and help lower intake of calories.

QUESTION 5

Correct Answer: All of the above

Any fruit or 100% fruit juice counts as part of the Fruit Group. Fruits may be fresh, canned, frozen, or dried, and may be whole, cut-up, or pureed.

QUESTION 6

Correct Answer: Maintaining proper bowel function

Eating foods that contain fiber – such as fruits, vegetables, and whole grains – may reduce risk for heart disease, protect against certain types of cancer, and help maintain proper bowel function.

QUESTION 7

Correct Answer: Folate

Folate is one of the B vitamins and is needed by all of our cells for growth. Although vitamin D and calcium are not typically found in high amounts in fruits, you can find some 100% orange juices that are fortified with calcium and vitamin D.

QUESTION 8

Correct Answer: Pepper

In plant biology, a fruit contains the seeds of a plant. Though it is botanically a fruit, a pepper counts toward the Vegetable Group because we eat peppers in a similar way to vegetables (on sandwiches, in soups, in pasta sauces). Likewise, tomatoes, squash, cucumbers, and pumpkins all contain the seeds of the plant and are therefore botanically fruits.

QUESTION 9

Correct Answer: All of the above

All fruits (and vegetables, too) contain some amount of vitamin C – an important nutrient that is needed for the growth and repair of tissues in all parts of your body.

QUESTION 10

Correct Answer: Fructose

Fructose is a natural sugar found in fruit that is responsible for the sweet flavor of many fruits.

Adapted from www.choosemyplate.gov/quiz. Accessed on June 29, 2018.

2. Read the quiz and its answers again. Then analyze the statements below and decide if they are true (T) or false (F). *Understanding details*

a. (   ) All fruits have high amounts of vitamin D and calcium.

b. (   ) Tomatoes and pumpkins are considered botanically fruits because they contain some amount of vitamin C.

c. (   ) Potassium can be found in several foods such as spinach, white beans, bananas, and low-fat milk.

d. (   ) Eating foods rich in fiber helps reduce risk for heart disease.

e. (   ) Fructose and pepper are important nutrients for the growth and repair of our body tissues.

EXPAND YOUR VOCABULARY

1. Refer back to the quiz and look for words or expressions to fit the definitions below.

a. _____: the amount of food, drink, etc, that you take into your body

b. _____: the soft inside part of a fruit or vegetable

c. _____: an illness which affects a person, animal, or plant

d. _____: the particular taste of a food or drink

e. _____: a natural substance such as iron that is present in some foods and is important for good health

Adapted from www.ldoceonline.com/dictionary/. Accessed on June 29, 2018.

2. Discuss the questions below with a classmate.

a. How important is it to learn about good nutrition?

b. What role do financial circumstances play in healthy eating habits?

c. What is the basic food intake pattern in Brazil based on?

d. If you could change one thing about your nutrition habits, what would it be? Why?

VOCABULARY IN USE

1. The Healthy Eating Plate was designed by nutrition experts at Harvard School of Public Health and editors at Harvard Health Publications. Use the words from the box to complete it.

   colors   butter   healthy protein   vegetables   coffee   white bread

   HEALTHY EATING PLATE

   Use healthy oils (like olive and canola oil) for cooking, on salad, and at the table. Limit _____. Avoid trans fat.

   The more veggies - and the greater the variety - the better. Potatoes and French fries don´t count.

   Eat plenty of fruits of all _____.

   STAY ACTIVE!
   © Harvard University

   Drink water, tea, or _____ (with little or no sugar). Limit milk/dairy (1-2 servings/day) and juice (1 small glass/day). Avoid sugary drinks.

   Eat a variety of whole grains (like whole-wheat bread, whole-grain pasta, and brown rice). Limit refined grains (like white rice and _____).

   Choose fish, poultry, beans, and nuts; limit red meat and cheese; avoid bacon, cold cuts, and other processed meats.

   Harvard T.H. Chan School of Public Health
   The Nutrition Source
   www.hsph.harvard.edu/nutritionsource

   Harvard Medical School
   Harvard Health Publications
   www.health.harvard.edu

   Extracted from www.hsph.harvard.edu/nutritionsource/healthy-eating-plate. Accessed on May 13, 2018.

2. Circle the best options to complete the statements about healthy eating according to the infographic in activity 1.

   a. One should restrict milk and dairy products such as **whole grain pasta and brown rice / cheese and butter** to one or two servings per day.

   b. **Olive and canola oils / Partially hydrogenated oils** are considered healthy oils.

   c. **Seafood and red meat / Bread and pasta**, mainly their wholegrain versions, are high in fiber, thus lowering one's risk of heart disease and constipation.

   d. **Lettuce, cabbage, and carrots / Fish, poultry, and beans** are examples of vegetables.

   e. Sodas, fruit juices, energy drinks, sugar-sweetened teas, and coffees are high in **added sugar and calories / carbohydrates and refined oils** and low in **fat / nutrients**.

3. Look at some other food items. Write their names under the correct headings.

Fruit & Vegetables	Proteins	Grains	Dairy

4. Compare your eating habits and the Healthy Eating Plate. Do you think the infographic reflects the reality of the region where you live? Justify your answer.

   _____

   _____

LANGUAGE IN USE 1

Unit 2

SIMPLE PRESENT – INTERROGATIVE FORM AND FREQUENCY ADVERBS

1. The questions below were extracted from the quiz on page 18. Read them and complete the statements about the simple present.

> "What **do** fruits **have** that make them sweet?"

> "Which fruit **is** this?"

> "Which of the following **counts** as part of the Fruit Group?"

a. The extracts on the left are in the _____ form.

b. To form interrogative sentences in the simple present, we use _____ when *I*, *you*, *we*, and *they* are the subject and *does* when *he*, *she*, and *it* are the subject.

c. For questions with the verb _____, we invert the position of the subject and the verb.

d. In subject questions, like the third one, there is no _____ verb and the word order is not inverted.

e. _____, *which*, *when*, *where*, and *how* are some question words that are used in information questions.

2. Now read the testimonials below carefully, paying attention to the words in bold, and choose the right alternative to complete the paragraph.

> "Every day your tip of the day pops up in my mailbox and I try to implement as many as possible. Making half my plate fruits and vegetables was my first mission. I don't **always** accomplish it, but I **always** try."
> Travis, South Dakota

> "I **never** ate a lot of leafy green things before my nutrition class this semester. Our teacher brought in kale and spinach and a few others and we each took one home. My Mom used one of your recipes and made a kale salad that I have to admit was actually really good! #GoMom"
> Kevin, New Hampshire

Adverbs like _____, *often*, *sometimes*, and _____, for example, are used to express the _____ of actions, to say how often we do things, or how often things happen. In general, frequency adverbs are positioned _____ main verbs but after the verb *be*.

a. ( ) always – far – frequency – after
b. ( ) always – never – frequency – before
c. ( ) often – always – time – before

Extracted from www.choosemyplate.gov/testimonials. Accessed on June 29, 2018.

3. Use the correct form of the verbs from the box to complete the questions from the Brazilian Dietary Guidelines.

| affect | be | broaden | derive | refer |

a. Besides the intake of nutrients, what else _____ diet _____ to?
Diet also refers to nutritious foods and how they are combined and prepared in meals.

b. _____ cultural and social dimensions of food choices _____ health and well-being?
Yes, and so do food preparation and modes of eating.

c. Where _____ healthy diets _____ from?
They derive from socially and environmentally sustainable food systems.

d. What _____ people's autonomy in food choices?
The access to respectable dietary recommendations.

e. _____ dietary patterns different in most countries?
Yes, they are. Especially in economically emerging countries.

Based on www.bvsms.saude.gov.br/bvs/publicacoes/dietary_guidelines_brazilian_population.pdf. Accessed on June 29, 2018.

EXPAND YOUR READING

1. **Read the text and circle the correct option.** *Skimming*
    a. The objective of the text is to show healthy recipes for teenagers.
    b. The text shows healthy tips for teenagers.
    c. The text presents a list of fruits and vegetables that teenagers can't eat.
    d. The objective of the text is to talk about ads and how they influence teenagers' diets.

 www.niddk.nih.gov/health-information/weight-management/take-charge-health-guide-teenagers

Take Charge of your Health: a Guide for Teenagers

Here are some helpful tips for making healthy eating decisions.

Many teens need more of these nutrients:

- Calcium, to build strong bones and teeth. Good sources of calcium are fat-free or low-fat milk, yogurt, and cheese.
- Vitamin D, to keep bones healthy. Good sources of vitamin D include orange juice, whole oranges, tuna, and fat-free or low-fat milk.
- Potassium, to help lower blood pressure. Try a banana, or **baked** potato with the skin, for a potassium boost.
- Fiber, to help you stay regular and feel full. Good sources of fiber include beans and **celery**.
- Protein, to power you up and help you grow strong. Peanut butter; eggs; tofu; legumes, such as lentils and peas; and chicken, fish, and low-fat meats are all good sources of protein.
- **Iron**, to help you grow. Red meat contains a form of iron that your body absorbs best. Spinach, beans, peas, and iron-fortified cereals are also sources of iron. You can help your body absorb the iron from these foods better when you also eat foods with vitamin C, like an orange.

Control your food portions

A portion is how much food or beverage you choose to consume at one time, whether in a restaurant, from a package, at school or a friend's, or at home. Many people consume larger portions than they need, especially when away from home.

Just one super-sized, fast food meal may have more calories than you need in a whole day. And when people are served more food, they may eat or drink more—even if they don't need it. This habit may lead to weight gain.

Adapted from www.niddk.nih.gov/health-information/weight-management/take-charge-health-guide-teenagers. Accessed on July 19, 2018.

---

2. **Read the text again and underline the correct options.**
    a. One of the main nutrients that teens need is **iron** / **vitamin E**.
    b. A good source of protein is **baked potato** / **fish**.
    c. Your body absorbs iron more easily if you eat foods with **vitamin C** / **vitamin D**.
    d. Eating one very large meal a day gives you **more** / **less** calories than you need in a whole day.
    e. **Spinach** / **Banana** is also a source of iron.
    f. **Protein** / **Calcium** helps to build strong teeth and bones.

LANGUAGE IN USE 2

Unit 2

OBJECT PRONOUNS

1. Below you will find some extracts from the text on page 22. Read them and answer the questions that follow.

   > [...]protein, to power **you** up and help **you** grow strong

   > **You** can help your body absorb the iron from these foods better when **you** also eat foods with vitamin C [...]

   > And when people are served more food, **they** may eat or drink more—even if **they** don't need **it**.

   a. In the first extract, is the pronoun *you* a subject or object of the sentence?

   _____

   b. How about in the second extract? Is the pronoun *you* the subject or the object of the sentence?

   _____

   c. In the third extract, what does the subject pronoun *they* refer to?

   _____

   d. In the third extract, is the pronoun *it* the subject or the object of the sentence? What does it refer to?

   _____

2. Read the paragraph and complete the table below with the object pronouns in bold.

   > My mom usually makes **me** lunch and she always makes sure that some of the food contains protein. She usually cooks red meat, because I love **it**! She also cooks some vegetables, like broccoli and carrots, but to be honest, I don't like **them** very much. Sometimes we have lunch together and I can tell **her** all about my day at school.

Subject pronouns	Object pronouns
I	
you	you
he	him
she	
it	
we	us
you	you
they	

3. Work in pairs. Circle the pronouns in the cartoon and discuss whether they are subject or object pronouns. Then share your opinions about the cartoon.

"Chocolate covered raisins, chocolate covered strawberries, chocolate covered cherries, and chocolate covered orange slices is not what I meant when I said that fruit is healthy for you."

Extracted from www.cartoonstock.com/cartoonview. asp?catref=aban1560. Accessed on May 14, 2018.

4. Read part of a news article called *Brazil has the best nutritional guidelines in the world* and choose the correct pronouns to complete it. Then work with a partner and discuss whether or not you agree with the idea it conveys.

   > Yesterday, a US-government appointed scientific panel released a 600-page report that will inform America's new dietary guidelines. These guidelines only come out every five years, and they matter because _____ (they / them) truly set the tone for how Americans eat: they're used by doctors and nutritionists to guide patient care, by schools to plan kids' lunches, and to calculate nutrition information on every food package you pick up, to name just a few areas of impact.
   >
   > But this panel and their guidelines too often overcomplicate what _____ (it / we) know about healthy eating. They take a rather punitive approach to food, reducing _____ (it / us) to its nutrient parts and emphasizing its relationship to obesity. Food is removed from the context of family and society and taken into the lab or clinic.
   >
   > Brazil, on the other hand, does exactly the opposite. Their national guidelines don't dwell on nutrients, calories, or weight loss. _____ (They / Them) don't jam foods into pyramids or child-like plates. Instead, they focus on meals and encourage citizens to simply cook whole foods at home, and to be critical of the seductive marketing practices of Big Food.
   >
   > The approach is so refreshing that _____ (me / it) has attracted praise from critics like Marion Nestle and Yoni Freedhoff, and when _____ (you / him) contrast the Brazilian method with the American way it's not hard to understand why.

   Adapted from www.vox.com/2015/2/20/8076961/brazil-food-guide. Accessed on June 29, 2018.

LISTENING COMPREHENSION

1. Work with a partner. Are nutritional guidelines different around the world? Exchange ideas and report your opinions to the class.

2. 🎧 03 Listen to the recording and check your answers to the question in activity 1. Were you right?

3. 🎧 04 Listen again and match the pictures with the nutritional guidelines they represent. Then go to the audio scripts on page 136 and check your answers.

| Germany | Guyana | Singapore | South Africa |

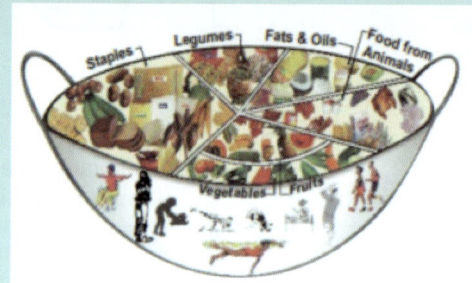

4. Based on the recording and on the discussions throughout the unit, come up with the ideal plate, considering all the possible variables for people your age. Then share your ideas with your classmates and teacher.

›› EXPAND YOUR HORIZONS ›››

Check (✔) the column that best describes your opinion about each statement. Then discuss your answers with your classmates and teacher, justifying your point of view.

	I agree.	I'm not sure.	I disagree.
a. Learning about healthy nutrition habits concerns everyone as it relates to cultural, social, political, and environmental issues.			
b. Natural, whole grain, gluten-free and organic may not always mean healthy alternatives.			
c. Dietary Guidelines should always reflect the local culture, prevention of diseases, healthy food and lifestyle, besides the importance of physical activity and weight management.			

REVIEW 1

Unit 1 and 2

1. Skim the text below and check (✓) the best option to complete the statement. *Skimming*

   The purpose of this text is...
   a. (   ) to inform the reader about eating habits in Brazil.
   b. (   ) to convince the reader to buy a book about eating customs in Brazil.

    http://thebrazilbusiness.com/article/dining-culture-in-brazil

   Cynthia Fujikawa Nes
   Co-Founder The Brazil Business

   Updated
   August 13, 2016

   ## Dining Culture in Brazil

   Brazilians are people who enjoy eating and like doing it a lot, even with only three meals. Here you will discover more about the Brazilian eating habits, such as tips on how to **behave** and cultural curiosities.

   5 Lunch time is sacred for Brazilians. They may think you are kidding if you say that you often just have a cold sandwich for lunch. A few hours after a light breakfast early in the morning – usually French bread and some coffee – people stream out of buildings ready to **tuck**
   10 **into** a large hot meal together with their coworkers.

   As most Brazilians will suggest, go to a *churrascaria* to have lunch. It is paradise for meat lovers. For those who are not familiar with the concept: *churrascaria* is a typical Brazilian steak house. At *churrascarias* with *rodízio* you will have
   15 waiters coming to your table with different types of meat on skewers which are carved at your table. There is usually salad and a buffet with hot dishes, so there is something for everybody in this type of restaurant. On your table you will find a disk: turn it green for a parade of meats to come
   20 to your table and red to stop it.

   Eating times in the afternoon are not a Brazilian habit, so do not expect to have a meal then. Some people drink coffee during this period, but since most Brazilians are working or doing some activity at this time of the
   25 day, they do not have time to stop and eat something of quality. A cereal bar, a chocolate bar, some candies, or potato chips are normally found in a Brazilian's bag or backpack. These items can be found in small stores usually located around office buildings.

   30 Dinner is the second main Brazilian meal and, more than lunch, is a family meal. Just like lunch, the Brazilian dinner is heavy and full of food, although it can be **obfuscated** by the goodies eaten in the afternoon.

   In terms of etiquette, the ideal thing to do is to wait
   35 until everybody has been served before starting eating, but it is accepted to start eating if the service is very slow. Brazilians use **cutlery** except for food like bread or boned chicken.

   Adapted from www.thebrazilbusiness.com/article/dining-culture-in-brazil. Accessed on July 17, 2018.

2. Underline the incorrect part in each sentence, according to the text. Then rewrite the sentences correcting them.

   a. Brazilians usually have only four meals.

   _____

   b. In Brazil, people usually have French bread and tea for breakfast.

   _____

   c. Churrascarias are typical Brazilian pasta houses.

   _____

   d. Brazilians have a meal in the afternoon. *Understanding details*

   _____

   e. The Brazilian dinner is light.

   _____

25

3. **Reread the text in activity 1 and find:**

   a. two frequency adverbs: _____ and _____.

   b. what the object pronoun *it* refers to in "turn *it* green for a parade of meats and red to stop", line 19: _____.

   c. what the subject pronoun *it* refers to in "*it* can be obfuscated by the goodies eaten in the afternoon", lines 31-32: _____.

   d. a suggestion in the affirmative form: _____.

   e. an instruction in the negative form: _____.

4. **Read part of the text "Brazil Should Do More for Venezuela's Refugees and Migrants" and fill in the blanks with the simple present of the verbs in parentheses.**

   ## Brazil Should Do More for Venezuela's Refugees and Migrants
   BY MARIA BEATRIZ BONNA NOGUEIRA AND MAIARA FOLLY | MARCH 20, 2017

   Over the past few months, thousands of Venezuelans have fled across the border to seek sanctuary in northern Brazil […] According to one recent arrival, Merlina Ferreira, "In Venezuela, I was a psychologist and my husband a lawyer. Here in Brazil, he _____ (unload) trucks and I _____ (look after) our small children since daycare _____ (be) too costly." Merlina _____ (join) at least 5,000 compatriots who recently applied for asylum in Boa Vista, a city in the state of Roraima. According to the Federal Police, the numbers **sky-rocketed** in the first few months of 2017, as compared to 2,230 applications in 2016, 234 in 2015, and just 9 in 2014. The spike in population displacement _____ (reflect) a dramatically deteriorating situation in Venezuela. Reports _____ (be) emerging of **spiraling** criminal violence, prolonged food shortages, and sustained unemployment. It _____ (be) still an open question whether these factors are legitimate grounds for refugee protection under international law. That hardly **matters** to people like Ferreira who _____ (feel) that their last resort to avoid starvation and homelessness is to cross an international border. Refugee specialist Alexander Betts _____ (describe) this phenomenon as "survival migration," and for good reason.

   Extracted from www.americasquarterly.org/content/brazil-should-do-more-venezuelas-refugees-and-migrants. Accessed on May 29, 2018.

5. **Complete the mind maps below with the words from the box.**

   citizenship   fiber   homeland   nutrition   fruit   persecution   policy   refugee   vegetables   whole grains

   IMMIGRATION

   HEALTHY EATING

UNIT 3
Your Digital Self

▶ **IN THIS UNIT YOU WILL...**
- talk about social media and big data;
- contrast the use of the present continuous and the simple present;
- learn how to use possessive adjectives;
- learn some common false cognates in English for Portuguese speakers.

LEAD OFF

- What social media services do you use?
- How much of your personal life do you usually share online?
- Why are social media networks so popular?

READING

❯❯ BEFORE READING — Relating to the topic

1. Rank the social media networks below 1-5 (1 = most used; 5 = least used) according to how often you use them. How similar or different is your ranking compared to your friends'?

   ____ Facebook   ____ Snapchat   ____ Instagram   ____ Twitter   ____ YouTube

2. Which of the following quotes do you mostly agree with? Why?

    a Smartphones and social media expand our universe. We can connect with others or collect information easier and faster than ever.
   Daniel Goleman

   Extracted from www.brainyquote.com/quotes/daniel_goleman_585902?src=t_social_media. Accessed on May 8, 2018.

    b It's so funny how social media was just this fun thing, and now it's this monster that consumes so many millennial lives.
   Cazzie David

   Extracted from www.brainyquote.com/quotes/cazzie_david_822611. Accessed on May 8, 2018.

❯❯ WHILE READING

Look at the snapshots of social media posts. What is each person doing?   *Scanning*

a. (   ) Sharing a disappointment.
b. (   ) Seeking advice from the community.
c. (   ) Celebrating an accomplishment.
d. (   ) Posting a recommendation.

1
RANDY SCHWARTZ
@randyscw Apr 7   [FOLLOW]

I am studying for my English exams. I am *struggling* with a couple of things, but I have no time to study everything. Gee… is using *proper* grammar on Twitter considered studying?

2 
YAY, Dude!
BFF
I'm so happy!!! In a few hours we're all traveling to play in the finals of the tournament!

3

♥ 42 likes

bittersweet Sometimes those you *trust* the most *bring you down*. I'm not feeling very well at the moment, and I don't know why I'm always making the same mistakes. People say time heals all, but the truth is that more

joycejjj Don't worry about that! I'm sure you *deserve* a lot more than that. Just give yourself time to *heal*.

3 DAYS AGO

4 
Diane W. B. Brown is at **The #1 Pizza Place** with **Amanda H.** and 4 others

OMG!!! I can't believe it's taken me this long to try this place! I'm having the best pizza EVER!!!! You guys should just stop whatever you're doing and try their pizza!! They aren't *kidding* about their name! It actually is the #1 pizza place on my list!! YUMMY!!

Unit 3

» AFTER READING

1. **Who would be likely to say the following sentences? Match the number of the text you read with each of the sentences below.** *Understanding main ideas*

   a. ( ) Next time I go out with my friends to grab a bite, I'm definitely coming back here!

   b. ( ) My life is so messed up at the moment that I don't know how long it'll take for me to get back on my feet.

   c. ( ) Well, they do say that you should try things out in real life if you really want learning to stick, right?

   d. ( ) I'm sure we're going to do well tomorrow! Everyone is feeling great about the game!

2. **Match the following replies with the texts you read.**

   a. ( ) I've already bought my tickets! I'm looking forward to seeing you all!! Go get 'em!

   b. ( ) Hey! I thought we were going there together! I'm so dying to get to know this place!

   c. ( ) Not sure what your point is. Maybe the best option is to focus on one thing at a time, don't you think?

   d. ( ) Don't let that hit you so hard! You'll soon notice that this is a great learning opportunity for you!

STUDY THIS

going to there → going there

EXPAND YOUR VOCABULARY

1. **Find the words or phrase in *italics* in the social media posts. Then match each of them with its meaning.**

   a. joking
   b. make you feel bad
   c. get what you should get because of your actions
   d. having difficulties
   e. an interjection of happiness and celebration
   f. correct, accurate
   g. believe, able to depend on
   h. helps in the recovery

   ( ) struggling
   ( ) proper
   ( ) yay
   ( ) trust
   ( ) bring you down
   ( ) heals
   ( ) deserve
   ( ) kidding

2. **Work in pairs. Discuss the questions below.**

   a. Have you ever heard of "big data"?

   b. What do you understand by this term? What does big data know about you?

   c. Is it possible not to leave a digital trail every time we use a computer, access our phones, or open up an app on a tablet? If so, how?

29

VOCABULARY IN USE

1. Some words in English are very similar to words in Portuguese, but they have different meanings. Look at the following sentence from text 4 and circle one word that is similar to Portuguese.

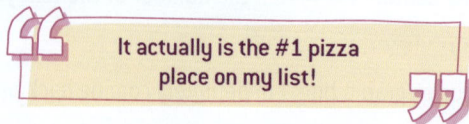
"It actually is the #1 pizza place on my list!"

The word *actually* in the sentence above is used because the author wants to emphasize her belief that that is the best pizza place in town. It has no reference to time. Words that seem similar in two languages, but that have different meanings are commonly known as *false friends*.

2. Match the false friends below with their correct definition.

   a. parents
   b. library
   c. assume
   d. balcony
   e. pretend
   f. push
   g. support
   h. assist
   i. notice
   j. fabric

   ( ) to help someone to do something
   ( ) to make someone or something move by pressing them with your hands, arms, etc.
   ( ) the mother and father of a person or animal
   ( ) to behave as if something is true when in fact you know it is not, in order to deceive people or for fun
   ( ) cloth used for making clothes, curtains, etc.
   ( ) a room or building containing books that can be looked at or borrowed
   ( ) approval, encouragement, and perhaps help for a person, idea, plan, etc.
   ( ) to think that something is true, although you do not have definite proof
   ( ) a structure that you can stand on, that is attached to the outside wall of a building, above ground level
   ( ) to realize that something or someone exists, especially because you can see, hear, or feel them

3. Use the words from activity 2 to complete the sentences below.

   a. I don't want to go to the movies with them, so I'll just _____ I'm busy.
   b. Susan really needs the _____ of her friends to win the competition.
   c. Can you _____ your brother with his homework?
   d. Mark _____ his sister and she fell on the floor.
   e. I _____ Facebook keeps track of everything we post there.
   f. You don't go to a _____ to buy books! You go to a bookstore!
   g. Jack has a nice _____ in his house where he keeps a hammock.
   h. Did you _____ that Google knows what you have searched for and makes suggestions based on that?
   i. Yes, my _____ are coming to visit for the holidays, but my siblings aren't.
   j. You can't find a better _____ than this for running T-shirts.

4. Do you know any other false friends? Come up with at least two more examples and write down sentences to illustrate their correct use.

   _____
   _____

LANGUAGE IN USE 1

Unit 3

PRESENT SIMPLE vs. PRESENT CONTINUOUS

1. Read these excerpts from the social media posts on page 28. Focus on the underlined words. Match the numbers with the meaning they convey.

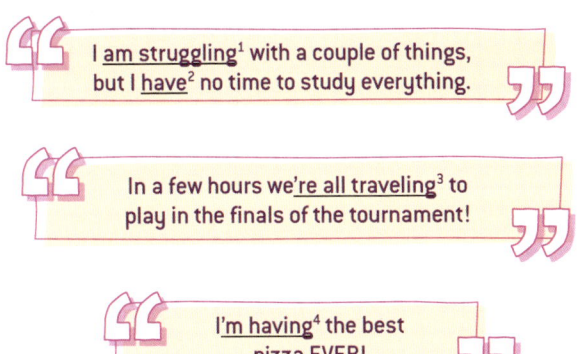

a. (   ) an action taking place at the moment of speech

b. (   ) a fact

c. (   ) an action that will happen in the future

d. (   ) an action that repeats itself constantly

2. Underline the correct option to complete each sentence.

a. I **don't usually share / am not usually sharing** lots of personal information on social media sites. However, today I **post / am posting** a picture of my birthday with my whole family.

b. Mark **enjoys / is enjoying** reading before going to bed, but he **doesn't do / isn't doing** that anymore because he **work / is working** a lot and he only **wants / is wanting** to sleep when he **gets / is getting** home.

c. Every time we **meet / are meeting** she **annoys / is annoying** me about getting a new hair cut.

d. Where **do you go / are you going** today after class? Can I come with you?

3. Complete the text with the appropriate verb form of the verbs in parentheses.

a. Tim _____ (wants / is wanting) to share what he _____ (does / is doing) right now with his friends from all over the world. He is a very popular boy, so he _____ (has / is having) many friends. Now he _____ (takes / is taking) pictures of his dog performing different tricks. However, he _____ (thinks / is thinking) about his privacy settings right now. Should he share the photos publicly or privately? He _____ (remembers / is remembering) what his parents told him: be careful with what you share online – it _____ (lives / is living) online forever!

b. Jane _____ (thinks / is thinking) about changing her phone, but she _____ (doesn't want / isn't wanting) to spend a lot of money. She _____ (likes / is liking) taking pictures, so it is important that the phone _____ (has / is having) a good camera. She also _____ (enjoys / is enjoying) spending hours on end talking to her friends on many messenger apps, so she _____ (needs / is needing) a phone with a good battery life. Actually, she _____ (has / is having) problems with her cell phone right now! She _____ (does / is doing) some research on what phone to buy, but the battery _____ (dies / is dying); she only has 15% left.

4. Rita is a teenager who uses social media a lot. In the extract below, she is explaining to her friend how she manages her Instagram account. Use the verbs from the box in the correct form to complete the passage. Use the negative form, if necessary.

  choose   edit (x2)   get   have   photoshop   want   work

OK, so this is how it _____. You _____ to share everything you do with everybody online. Sometimes, I _____ photos that I only want to share with my close friends, like, it's my inner thoughts and my real self, and other times there are photos I want everyone to see. Let me show you... here... I _____ a photo to post to my *rinsta*, which is my real Instagram account, the one with all the edited photos and open to all. I _____ the photo because I really want it to look good so I _____ more likes. However, the photos that go onto my *finsta*, which is the account I share only with my closest friends, are a lot less edited. I mean, I usually _____ the photos that go there, but this one in particular I _____ because I want to blur the face of that woman behind me.

EXPAND YOUR READING

1. Read the passages below and decide if each person is talking about one of the pros (P) or cons (C) of social media.
   a. ( ) My sister's best friend is studying abroad. They hate the distance, but at least they can keep their communication up to date through the use of the Internet.
   b. ( ) I have a big test tomorrow, but my friends want me to join them in this online LOL competition. I think my grades are going to suffer a lot, but I can't help it! We are on our way to the regional finals and we have to play.
   c. ( ) Jack had been offered a great job from a company, but the offer was withdrawn after a quick search of his timeline.
   d. ( ) Mrs. Wilson is just the best! Her knowledge of social media and willingness to integrate that into her lessons makes it a lot easier for kids to focus on their tasks!

Raising a Teenager in the Digital Age

It seems like the Internet just came out of nowhere and changed everything, including childhood. Whether this change has been for the better or worse depends on how you look at it.

Teens today are the first generation that cannot imagine life without the Internet and the various devices that connect us to it. *Our* electronic gadgets have become extensions of our bodies, like crutches. On the other hand, you might also say that these powerful tools give us wings. Some people believe that the Internet and *its* various social networking options affect us negatively while others beg to differ. Parents who cling to their pre-Internet way of life are scrambling to make sure they have the right answers to guide *their* kids.

CONS
- Heavy social media use can possibly lead to depression, anxiety, and low self-esteem.
- It can prevent the development of some social and direct communication skills.
- Can **embolden** people to **harass** others online.
- Can be a major distraction for students and can lead to poor academic performance.
- Some inappropriate posts may hurt job opportunities down the line.

PROS
- Can **provide** a platform for shy people to express themselves and boost their confidence.
- Can facilitate communication between those that are marginalized.
- Can **strengthen** and maintain relationships to friends close and far.
- Classrooms can use social media to keep students engaged with study materials and lessons.
- A healthy social media presence can be beneficial in attracting employers.

Adapted from www.wehavekids.com/parenting/social-network-to-teens. Accessed on May 11, 2018.

2. Underline the correct option to complete the statements according to the text you have just read.
   a. Social media **can make it easier / make it harder** for people who are shy to express their thoughts.
   b. Bullies might feel **stronger / weaker** because of the anonymity that the Internet provides.
   c. If you use it correctly, social media can actually **hinder / help** with the chances of landing a new job.
   d. People who use social media a lot **may / may not** have difficulties dealing with real-life encounters.
   e. Social media is **only / also** great for people to keep in touch with their friends who live far away.

LANGUAGE IN USE 2

Unit 3

POSSESSIVE ADJECTIVES

1. Read the sentence below and check (✓) the correct sentence.

> "John went to the club with his friend and her mother."

In the sentence above, we can say that the following people went to the club:

a. ( ) One man and two women.
b. ( ) One man, one woman, and one person who can be a man or a woman.
c. ( ) Two men and one woman.

2. Circle the correct option to complete the rules below.
   a. The possessive adjective comes **before** / **after** the noun.
   b. We **use** / **do not use** articles when we use a possessive adjective.

Go back to activity 1 on page 32 and complete the table with the possessive adjectives in italics.

Subject Pronouns	Possessive Adjective
I	my
you	your
he	his
she	her
it	
we	
you	your
they	

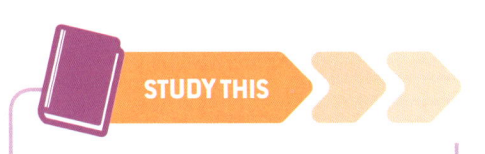

STUDY THIS

Even though the word *friend* can be used either for a man or a woman, in the sentence in activity 1, the possessive adjective before the word *mother* refers back to the word *friend*. In English, all possessive adjectives make reference to the possessor, not to the object or person that the they are describing. Consequently, when we say *her mother*, we know that the friend is a woman because of the possessive adjective that was used: HER.

3. Complete the sentences below with the correct possessive adjective.
   a. I am playing *League of Legends* and I am talking to _____ friends online. We need to come up with _____ strategy to win the game.
   b. Our friends asked _____ parents if they could come to the movie theater with us.
   c. What social media site/network do you use the most to share _____ pictures?
   d. Facebook has decided to change _____ privacy rules again.
   e. What is _____ opinion about Snapchat? Do you think it is still the number one social media app for teenagers, or do they use Instagram for _____ stories now?
   f. Jenny is going to ask_____ dad if _____ friends are also taking _____ children to the party so that she knows there'll be someone _____ age there as well.
   g. My cousin Josh and _____ dad are taking cooking lessons and _____ teacher is a famous chef from London. How great is that?
   h. Last week I posted _____ birthday pictures on Instagram. I love the fact that we can use social media as an online photo album.

33

LISTENING COMPREHENSION

1. **Work in pairs and discuss the questions below.**
   a. How concerned are you about your privacy online?
   b. How do social media platforms make money?
   c. Can you think of an alternative way for them to make money?

2. **You will hear five different extracts about social media networks and how people use them. Match each extract (1–5) with one of the opinions below.**

   05
   a. (   ) We need to think about both the pros and the cons of social media any time we log on to one of these sites.
   b. (   ) Some media sites are great tools and we don't need to feel guilty about using them.
   c. (   ) It is difficult for competitors to deal with social media giants these days.
   d. (   ) There is a lot of talk about innovation, but the social media landscape is not innovative at the moment.
   e. (   ) Just like it happened with cars and paint, social networks need to offer safety tools.

3. **Go to the audio script on page 136 and check your answers. Then do the activities that follow.**
   a. Choose three words or phrases from the audio scripts that you would like to learn.
   b. Ask your friends if they know the meaning of the words you have chosen.
   c. Write down one original sentence using each one of the words or phrases.

   _____
   _____
   _____
   _____
   _____
   _____

>> EXPAND YOUR HORIZONS >>>>

Check (✓) the column that best describes your opinion about each statement. Then discuss your answers with your classmates and teacher, justifying your point of view.

	I agree.	I'm not sure.	I disagree.
a. More and more consumer products will be launched on social media due to all the personal information people give away.			
b. As more and more users buy likes and followers on Instagram, influencer marketing through social media will become more difficult.			
c. In the near future, regardless of their job title, people will need to adapt to the online social sphere in order to be successful.			

UNIT 4
Establishing and Keeping Relationships

▶ IN THIS UNIT YOU WILL…

- talk about how teens relate to others;
- exchange ideas about different types of relationships;
- express opinions about building and maintaining relationships at all levels;
- use the simple past to talk about finished actions, events, or states in the past;
- use the modal verbs *can* and *should*.

LEAD OFF

- What is the relationship among the people in the picture? What makes you think so?
- How important is it to build and maintain good relationships in life?
- How do you relate to others?

READING

›› BEFORE READING

Discuss the quote below in pairs. Then report your opinions to the class. *Bridging and relating to the topic*

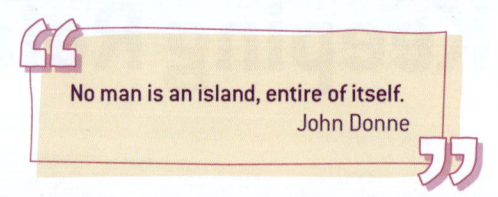

> "No man is an island, entire of itself.
> John Donne"

Extracted from www.goodreads.com/work/quotes/6791114-no-man-is-an-island. Accessed on May 16, 2018.

›› WHILE READING

1. Read the title of the magazine article in activity 2. What do you expect to read about? *Predicting*

2. Who are more emotional, teens or adults? How can we build better relationships? Read the text below and understand how relationships change from childhood to adulthood.

How the Teen Brain Transforms Relationships

BY DANIEL SIEGEL | AUGUST 12, 2014

1. More intense emotion

As a child approaches adolescence, his or her emotions become more intense.
One study, for example, put kids, adolescents, and adults into a brain scanner and showed them a picture of an emotionally expressive or neutral face. They found more intense emotional responses among adolescents, and a relatively mild response among both the kids and adults.
The **downside** of this increased emotionality is that teens can become more easily irritated, upset, and moody—and they can have a relationship with themselves that's confusing.

2. Risk and novelty becomes more compelling

Compared to a kid or an adult, the baseline levels of dopamine in an adolescent are lower. But the **release** amounts are higher—and novelty is one of the major things that can **trigger** dopamine release. This means new things feel really, really good to a teenager. This is brilliant. Nature has created a system that drives us to seek change and novelty, a push for the unfamiliar and even the uncertain, which is what a teen must do if they're ever going to get out of the house.
But there's a downside, of course: What happens when dopamine levels drop? The teen gets bored with the same old, same old.

3. We seek attachment in peers

We mammals have attachment, which is built on four childhood needs: to be seen, safe, **soothed**, and secure. What happens with attachment in the early years is really important because infants depend on their **caregivers** to survive.
But as we grow older, attachment doesn't go away—it's a lifelong process. What happens when you're a kid moving into adolescence? What do you do with your attachment needs? Instead of turning only toward your parents, you start turning to your peers more, which is a very healthy thing to do.
One really big downside is that membership in an adolescent **peer** group—even if it's just one other person—can feel like a matter of life and death: "If I don't have at least one peer that I'm connected with, I'm gonna die." That's what millions and millions of years of evolution are telling this adolescent.
We need that closeness for another reason that goes well beyond just one party, which is that, given the psychological stakes, teens can sacrifice morality for membership. We have a name for that: peer pressure.
So what parents and teens need to do, together, is cultivate the upside of this shift from parents to peers as attachment figures. If you spend your adolescence developing social skills, your adulthood is going to be so much better.

Adapted from www.greatergood.berkeley.edu/article/item/how_the_teen_brain_transforms_relationships. Accessed on May 16, 2018.

AFTER READING

1. Refer back to the question in activity 1 on page 36. Were your predictions correct? Talk to a classmate and explain your answer. `Checking predictions`

2. Underline the correct statements according to the magazine article. `Understanding details`
   a. The study found more emotional responses among teenagers than adults and children.
   b. When dopamine levels drop, teenagers tend to stick to their safe old habits.
   c. Peer pressure is the pressure you feel to behave in the way that your family expects you to.
   d. Mammals feel that connecting with a peer group can be a matter of survival.

3. Work in groups to discuss the following questions.
   a. Are teens' relationships today different from past generations'?
   b. Has the Internet affected any sorts of relationships? How?
   c. To what extent do aspects such as finances, social level, affinities, and schooling interfere with the relationships you build?

EXPAND YOUR VOCABULARY

1. Go through the article on page 36 again and find:
   a. a synonym for *adolescent*: _____;
   b. three stages in one's existence: _____, _____, and _____;
   c. three adjectives often attributed to teens on increased emotionality: _____, _____, and _____;
   d. four childhood needs: _____;
   e. a neurotransmitter that is triggered by novelty, among other things: _____;
   f. an opposite of *aversion, disconnection*: _____.

2. Check (✔) the correct meaning of the words and expressions in bold in the extracts below according to the context.
   a. What happens when dopamine levels drop? The teen gets bored with the **same old, same old**.
      ( ) used to describe a fun, exciting event
      ( ) used to say that a situation has not changed, when this is boring or annoying
   b. "Nature has created a system that **drives** us to seek change and novelty, a push for the unfamiliar and even the uncertain, [...]"
      ( ) strongly influences
      ( ) makes a car move along
   c. "We need that closeness for another reason that goes well beyond just one party, which is that, given the psychological **stakes**, [...]"
      ( ) boundary marks such as sticks or posts pointed at one end
      ( ) risks or investments
   d. "So what parents and teens need to do, together, is cultivate the **upside** of this shift from parents to peers as attachment figures."
      ( ) the positive part of a usually bad situation
      ( ) the upper side or part of something

3. Use at least three words and expressions listed in activities 1 and 2 to finish the paragraph below.

   In my opinion, the role of relationships in teenage life...
   _____
   _____
   _____
   _____
   _____
   _____

Unit 4

37

VOCABULARY IN USE

1. Go back to the text on page 36 and search for the phrasal verb whose meaning is "leave a place or a person".

2. The phrasal verbs below refer to relationships at all levels. Match them with their definitions.

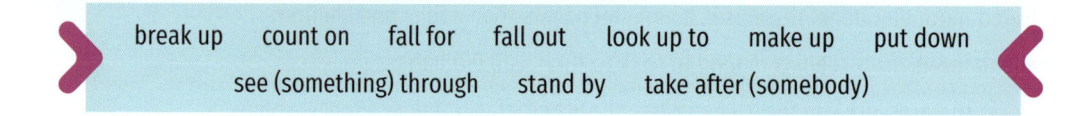

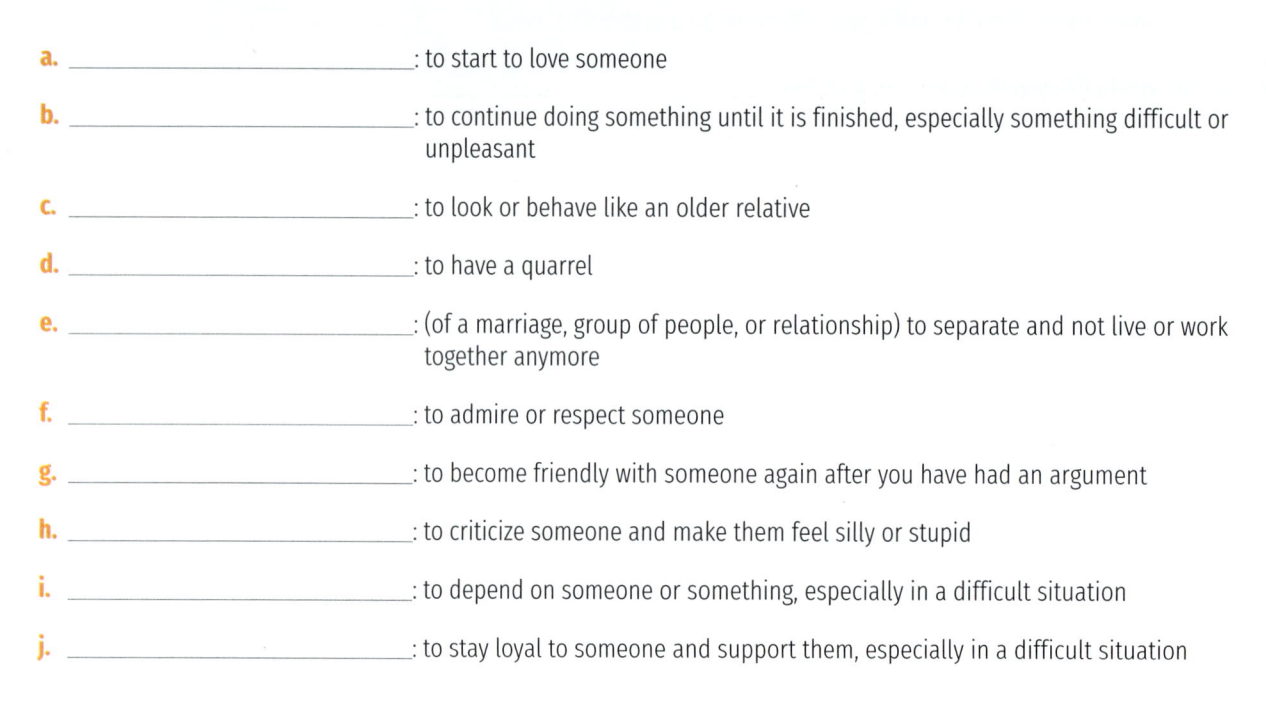

> break up   count on   fall for   fall out   look up to   make up   put down
> see (something) through   stand by   take after (somebody)

a. _____: to start to love someone

b. _____: to continue doing something until it is finished, especially something difficult or unpleasant

c. _____: to look or behave like an older relative

d. _____: to have a quarrel

e. _____: (of a marriage, group of people, or relationship) to separate and not live or work together anymore

f. _____: to admire or respect someone

g. _____: to become friendly with someone again after you have had an argument

h. _____: to criticize someone and make them feel silly or stupid

i. _____: to depend on someone or something, especially in a difficult situation

j. _____: to stay loyal to someone and support them, especially in a difficult situation

Extracted from www.ldoceonline.com/. Accessed on June 28, 2018.

3. Use some of the phrasal verbs from activity 2 to complete the quotes below. Then talk to a classmate about what they mean and say if you agree with them.

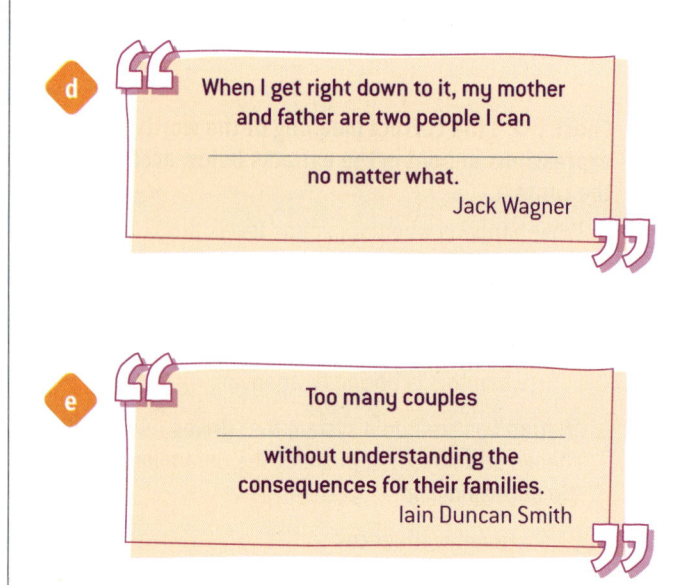

a. "I want to _____ my country, but I cannot vote for war."
   Jeannette Rankin

b. "It hurts when people _____ you _____."
   Timbaland

c. "It's good for kids to _____ sporting role models."
   Adam Peaty

d. "When I get right down to it, my mother and father are two people I can _____ no matter what."
   Jack Wagner

e. "Too many couples _____ without understanding the consequences for their families."
   Iain Duncan Smith

Extracted from www.brainyquote.com. Accessed on July 16, 2018.

LANGUAGE IN USE 1

Unit 4

SIMPLE PAST

1. The excerpt below was extracted from the article on page 36. Read it and check (✓) the correct answer to the question that follows.

> One study, for example, **put** kids, adolescents, and adults into a brain scanner and **showed** them a picture of an emotionally expressive or neutral face. They **found** more intense emotional responses among adolescents, and a relatively mild response among both the kids and adults.

Why is the simple past used in this fragment of the article?

( ) Because it is about facts that are happening at the moment.

( ) Because this part of the text talks about completed actions in the past.

2. Reread the excerpt in activity 1 and complete the sentences about the simple past.

a. The _____ is used to talk about _____ actions, events, and states that happened at a specific time in the past.

b. _____ is an example of a regular verb in the past. In the simple past, regular verbs end in _____.

c. _____ and _____ are examples of irregular verbs in the past. Irregular verbs don't follow any specific spelling rules in the simple past.

3. Now read the questions and answers based on the extracts from activity 1 and make more deductions about the simple past.

> **Were** adults part of the study?
> Yes, they **were**.

> **Did** they **find** more intense emotional responses among the kids and adults?
> No, they **didn't**.

> What **did** the researchers **show** kids, adolescents, and adults in the study?
> They **showed** them a picture of an emotionally expressive or neutral face.

a. While in _____ sentences the past forms of the verb are used, in interrogative and negative forms we use the auxiliaries _____ and _____ respectively and the verb is in its base form.

b. The past forms of the verb *be* are *was* and _____. For short answers we use *Yes / No* followed by the _____ and *was, were / wasn't, weren't*.

4. Use the verbs in parentheses in the affirmative form of the simple past to complete the poem below.

> **Love And Friendship**
> A poem by George Bernard Shaw
>
> Have you told your kids I love you?
> Given them all a big hug today?
> In my youth loving words _____ (be) few,
> We were sent out to be out of the way.
> Indoors we _____ (speak) when spoken to,
> Silence _____ (rule) most of our day.
> When breaking a rule we always _____ (know),
> That punishment would come our way.
> Each _____ (have) their jobs of work to be done,
> We _____ (clean) and polished and _____ (shine).
> Life believe me _____ (be) not much fun,
> For breach of the rules we were fined.
> In the orphanage no one _____ (say) I love you,
> Never the time for a hug and a kiss,
> Friendship _____ (be) for me something new,
> It was the main thing that I did most miss.
> So remember to hug and kiss your kids each day,
> Show them that you love and care.
> That they too will go on their way,
> With love and friendship to share.

Extracted from www.poemhunter.com/poems/friendship/page-1/263674. Accessed on May 19, 2018.

EXPAND YOUR READING

1. Read the texts and check the correct option to complete the sentence.

   Cathy November 18, 2010

   Drabble November 16, 2012

   JumpStart June 10, 2010

   Extracted from https://assets.amuniversal.com. Accessed on May 19, 2018.

   Comic strips...

   ( ) present words and are seen in books or newspapers. They describe the pictures and explain what they show.

   ( ) present a series of pictures, usually organized horizontally, designed as a narrative or a chronological sequence.

2. Circle the correct options to complete the characteristics of comic strips.
   Comic strips...
   a. are generally **humorous** / **serious** and sometimes have a moral.
   b. use graphic conventions such as **speech and thought bubbles** / **captions** and punctuation signs in the text.
   c. employ visual arrangements to tell a story and often reproduce **formal** / **oral** language.
   d. are written in **lower case** / **capital** letters most of the times.
   e. **never** / **usually** use facial expressions and gestures to show action and thoughts.

3. Work in pairs. What kinds of relationship do the comic strips present?

LANGUAGE IN USE 2

Unit 4

MODAL VERBS — CAN and SHOULD

1. Read some extracts from the comics on page 40 and statements about them. Decide if the statements are true (T) or false (F). Correct the false ones.

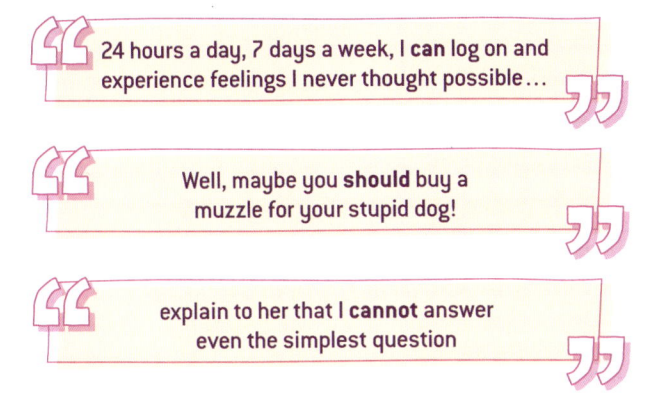

   > 24 hours a day, 7 days a week, I **can** log on and experience feelings I never thought possible…

   > Well, maybe you **should** buy a muzzle for your stupid dog!

   > explain to her that I **cannot** answer even the simplest question

   > **Can** you at least remind me what her name is?

   a. ( ) In the first extract, *can* expresses ability.

   b. ( ) The modal *should* used in the second extract indicates a piece of advice.

   c. ( ) In the third extract, *cannot* means *not able to*.

   d. ( ) In the fourth extract, *can* is used to ask what is probable to happen.

2. Read the comic strip below and answer the question in pairs. Then share your opinions about it. In the first and second panels of the strip, is *can* used for possibility or permission?

   Baldo   September 09, 2010

   Extracted from www.assets.amuniversal.com/7a5c2fa0ca650131604c005056a9545dw. Accessed on May 20, 2018.

3. Choose the correct option to complete the comics.

   Calvin and Hobbes   February 26, 1990

   Extracted from www.assets.amuniversal.com/6ac251f0dece013171ac005056a9545dw. Accessed on May 20, 2018.

   a. ( ) can I go / should I stay / can things be

   b. ( ) should I go / can't I stay / can't things be

LISTENING COMPREHENSION

1. It's common sense that respect is mandatory in all sorts of relationships. But what happens with lack of respect? Have you seen or experienced situations of disrespect in relationships? Share your answers.

2. Below is a poster from a campaign held by *The Diana Award*, an independent British charity whose aim is to empower young people to change the world. What kind of campaign is it?

BACK_2 SCHOOL

FROM THE DIANA AWARD ANTI-BULLYING CAMPAIGN

Extracted from www.youtube.com/watch?v=F3kR5fwscg4. Accessed on May 20, 2018.

3. Listen to Danny Boy and choose the correct options to complete the sentences.

   06

   a. Danny Boy is...
      ( ) a former victim of bullying.
      ( ) a former bully.

   b. According to Danny Boy, ...
      ( ) one should control other people's lives.
      ( ) one should control his/her own life.

   c. Danny Boy used to feel scared...
      ( ) so he decided to go to his friend's house.
      ( ) and wanted to avoid the person who habitually intimidated him.

   d. Danny Boy says the bullied should (select two)...
      ( ) call the police immediately.
      ( ) approach the ones who like them.
      ( ) open up and talk to people.
      ( ) join a therapy group.

4. Work in small groups. Discuss the questions below with your classmates. Then report your answers to the class.

   a. What other damages can be caused when people disrespect and violate the standards of good relationships?

   b. When you come across a conflict in a relationship, how do you usually cope with it?

   c. Do all countries have the same cultural values regarding relationships at all levels? Justify your answer.

>> EXPAND YOUR HORIZONS >>>>

Check (✓) the column that best describes your opinion about each statement. Then discuss your answers with your classmates and teacher, justifying your point of view.

	I agree.	I'm not sure.	I disagree.
a. Compromise is a crucial part of a relationship. Everyone should make sacrifices for the sake of relating to others effectively.			
b. Understanding the background of the people you relate to helps maintain healthy relationships at all levels.			
c. Communication, acceptance, and respect are inherited traits of any good relationship and the lack of those may bring about serious damage to people.			

REVIEW 2

Unit 3 and 4

1. Read the title of the text below. What do you expect to read about? *Predicting*

The problems of big data, and what to do about them

In the last 15 years, we have **witnessed** an explosion in the amount of digital data available – from the Internet, social media, scientific equipment, smart phones, surveillance cameras, and many other sources – and in the computer technologies used to process it. "Big Data," as it is known, will **undoubtedly** deliver important scientific, technological, and medical advances. But Big Data also poses serious risks if it is misused or abused.

5 Already, major innovations such as Internet search engines, machine translation, and image labeling have relied on applying machine-learning techniques to vast data sets. And, in the near future, Big Data could significantly improve government policymaking, social-welfare programs, and **scholarship**.

But having more data is no substitute for having high-quality data. For example, a recent article in *Nature* reports that election pollsters in the United States are struggling to obtain representative samples of the population, because they are 10 legally permitted to call only landline telephones, whereas Americans increasingly rely on cell phones. [...]

In recent years, automated programs based on biased data sets have caused numerous scandals. For example, last April, when a college student searched Google images for "unprofessional hairstyles for work," the results showed mostly pictures of black people; when the student changed the first search term to "professional," Google returned mostly pictures of white people. [...]

Another **hazard** of Big Data is that it can be gamed. When people know that a data set is being used to make important 15 decisions that will affect them, they have an incentive to tip the scales in their favor. [...]

A third hazard is privacy violations, because so much of the data now available contains personal information. In recent years, enormous collections of confidential data have been stolen from commercial and government sites; and researchers have shown how people's political opinions or even sexual preferences can be accurately gleaned from seemingly innocuous online postings, such as movie reviews – even when they are published pseudonymously.

20 Finally, Big Data poses a challenge for **accountability**. Someone who feels that he or she has been treated **unfairly** by an algorithm's decision often has no way to appeal it, either because specific results cannot be interpreted, or because the people who have written the algorithm refuse to provide details about how it works. [...]

The good news is that the hazards of Big Data can be largely avoided. But they won't be unless we **zealously** protect people's privacy, detect and correct unfairness, use algorithmic recommendations prudently, and maintain a rigorous understanding of algorithms' inner workings and the data that informs their decisions.

Extracted from www.weforum.org/agenda/2017/02/big-data-how-we-can-manage-the-risks. Accessed on June 04, 2018.

2. Read the text in activity 1 and check the most appropriate definition for Big Data. *Making inferences*

   a. ( ) a system of connecting computers to the Internet and moving information, such as messages or pictures, at a very high speed

   b. ( ) the very large amounts of information that can now be gathered, kept, and analyzed, especially information about people's interests or what they like, as a result of things such as social media use

   Adapted from www.ldoceonline.com/. Accessed on June 28, 2018.

3. Mention two risks posed if Big Data is misused or abused, according to the text. *Understanding details*

   _____
   _____
   _____

4. Read an extract from the text. Circle the sentence that refers to a fact and underline the sentence that refers to an action taking place at the moment the text was written.

   "[...]

   But having more data is no substitute for having high-quality data. For example, a recent article in *Nature* reports that election pollsters in the United States are struggling to obtain representative samples of the population, because they are legally permitted to call only landline telephones, whereas Americans increasingly rely on cellphones.

   [...]"

5. Choose the correct option to complete the paragraph.

> We _____ in a digital age, so technology is definitely a part of our daily life. Teens _____ social media platforms such as Facebook, Instagram, and Twitter to express themselves and to look for information as well. In fact, teens _____ always _____ the virtual world to communicate with one another. It's also true that most teens _____ to one site; they often _____ and end up using multiple ones.

- **a.** ( ) are living / are accessing / are... using / doesn't stick / are experimenting
- **b.** ( ) live / access / are... using / don't stick / are experimenting
- **c.** ( ) live / are accessing / are... using / don't stick / experiment

6. Use the cues from the box to complete the quotes. There is an extra option which you do not need to use.

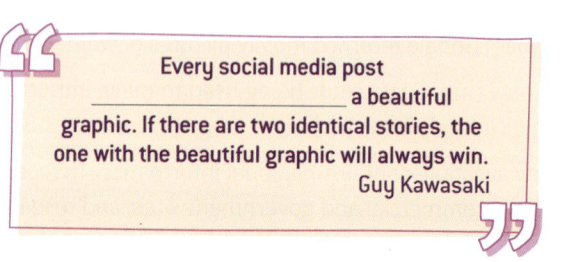

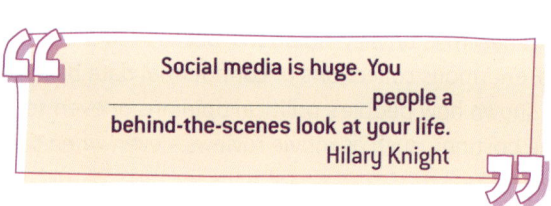

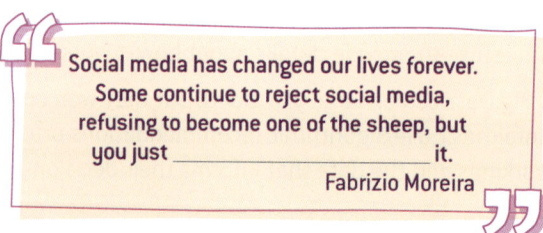

> shouldn't do   can give   can't avoid   should have

> "Every social media post _____ a beautiful graphic. If there are two identical stories, the one with the beautiful graphic will always win."
> Guy Kawasaki

> "Social media is huge. You _____ people a behind-the-scenes look at your life."
> Hilary Knight

> "Social media has changed our lives forever. Some continue to reject social media, refusing to become one of the sheep, but you just _____ it."
> Fabrizio Moreira

Extracted from www.brainyquote.com. Accessed on September 21, 2018.

7. Fill in the blanks in the comic strip with the simple past of the verbs *be*, *transform*, and *turn*.

JumpStart   February 24, 2011   ID: 283486

Extracted from https://assets.amuniversal.com/01fb6fe01b37012ea5c900163e41dd5bw. Accessed on June 5, 2018.

UNIT 5
Art: The Language of Emotions

▶ IN THIS UNIT YOU WILL...
- talk about different forms of art;
- learn how to form words using prefixes;
- understand the formation of plural nouns;
- learn the correct order of adjectives when describing a noun.

LEAD OFF
> What comes to your mind when you think of art?
> What do you see in the picture?
> What do you think the author of this picture wanted to express? Which themes are depicted in the picture?

READING

▶▶ BEFORE READING — Relating to the topic

1. Art comes in different forms and can be found in different places. Look at the pictures and identify where you would most likely find these examples of art.

a ( ) on the streets   b ( ) in a museum   c ( ) in an art gallery   d ( ) at an event

2. What do you think of the following quote? How much do you agree with it?

> "The purpose of art is washing the dust of daily life off our souls.
> Pablo Picasso"

▶▶ WHILE READING

Read the article and decide if the statements are true (T) or false (F).   *Scanning*

a. ( ) Art is only art if it is in a museum.
b. ( ) Any place can be a possible site for art.
c. ( ) One of the goals of art is to engage a community.
d. ( ) Creativity is not innate in human beings.

www.artsy.net/article/artsy-editorial-the-most-relevant-art-today-is-taking-place-outside-the-art-world

The Most Relevant Art Today Is Taking Place Outside the Art World

[…] If you walk east from Columbia's Butler Library, down the rocky hills of Morningside Park, and cross a few avenues, you will find a relatively *nondescript* **laundromat**, one of some 3,000 in New York. It's not a gallery, nor *a pop-up space*, nor the work of an artist who turned an abandoned building into a functioning laundromat. No, it's a laundromat, but *nonetheless* one *bursting* with creativity.

5 […] During the summer months, it *hosts* workshops by The Laundromat Project, a nonprofit officially started in 2005 that **seeks** to "amplify the creativity that already exists within communities" through residencies, development programs, and a host of other events, as its executive director Kemi Ilesanmi explained to me. The benefit of hosting public events in laundromats is engaging a diverse group of people. In New York, at least, they are "multi-generational, multi-race, and multi-class spaces," says Ilesanmi. The type of community engagement *fostered* by the
10 project isn't about painting a mural and walking away, but rather commissioning artists who think long and hard about how to engage the communities where the project operates: Harlem, Bedford Stuyvesant, and Hunts Point/Longwood, three neighborhoods primarily made up of people of color with modest incomes and rich histories. […]

"One of the things that makes us *stand out* is that we meet people where they are," said Ilesanmi. "It's not that museums can't or have never done that. But we actually do it all the time. It's not a special project. […] In our opinion everyone is
15 creative, and we remind them of that even when they don't think that about themselves," said Ilesanmi, adding, "creative expression is just a part of being human beings." As we spoke, she talked through the imagined voice of any given person: "I dance, I love music, I love "fill in the blank", as a human being in the world. However, I don't need that validated by, nor do I feel like I have to go into, a formal setting." Likely because of this inclusive approach, the Laundromat Project has been met with success. The organization was featured at the Creative Time **summit** and successfully raised $35,000
20 in 10 days this year. It's now thinking about how it will adapt and change its program in the future.

Extracted from www.artsy.net/article/artsy-editorial-the-most-relevant-art-today-is-taking-place-outside-the-art-world. Accessed on June 12, 2018.

Unit 5

›› AFTER READING

1. What are your interpretations for the pieces of art below? Match the numbers with the pictures.

  a. to reflect about conflict

  b. to reflect about conformity

  c. to reflect about human identity

( ) ( ) ( )

Head in the Box, 1979-81, Peter Wilson   Rage, the Flower Thrower, 2005, Banksy   Cape Cod Evening, 1939, Edward Hopper

2. Underline the incorrect information in each statement according to the article. *Understanding details*

  a. Most people are creative and the Laundromat Project accepts this as a universal truth.

  b. The Laundromat project has certainly been successful because of its inclusive approach.

  c. The Laundromat project reminds people of how creative they are only if they think that about themselves.

  d. Only a specific group of people is engaged with art in the Laundromat project.

3. Rewrite the statements from activity 2 with the correct information.

  a. _____

  b. _____

  c. _____

  d. _____

EXPAND YOUR VOCABULARY

1. Find the words or expressions in *italics* in the reading. Then match each one with its meaning.

  a. helped a skill, feeling, idea, etc, develop over a period of time

  b. so full that nothing else can fit inside

  c. opened somewhere for a short, limited period of time

  d. looking very ordinary and not at all interesting

  e. to be much better than other similar people or things

  f. in spite of the fact that has just been mentioned

  g. to provide the place and everything that is needed for an organized event

( ) nondescript

( ) a pop-up space

( ) nonetheless

( ) bursting

( ) host

( ) fostered

( ) stand out

2. Is there any space in your city that is used, or could be used, to host such an event? Are the people who live in your city creative? How do (or would) they benefit from such a space to express their art?

VOCABULARY IN USE

1. The prefix *non-* is added to the beginning of the word *profit* to create a new word in meaning: *nonprofit*. Read the examples of the most common prefixes and complete the table with the words *possible* and *ordinary*, adding the correct prefix to them.

Prefix	Meaning	Example
anti-	against / opposed to	anti-government
dis-	reverse or remove	disagree
down-	reduce or lower	downgrade
extra-	beyond	_____
il- / im- / in- / ir-	not	illegal _____ insecure irregular
mis-	incorrectly	misspelled
non-	not	nonpayment
re-	again	redo
co-	together, mutually	co-worker

2. Circle the prefix in the words below.

   a. dishonest
   b. redo
   c. illiterate
   d. extraterrestrial
   e. non-smoking
   f. irresponsible
   g. misbehave
   h. downhearted
   i. incapable
   j. anti-racist
   k. immigrate

3. Complete the sentences with a word from activity 2.
   a. My grade was extremely low, so my teacher told me to _____ my essay.
   b. Brian was _____ because his friend was moving away.
   c. It was _____ of you to leave her alone.
   d. The city's road system is _____ of handling such a volume of traffic.
   e. How do scientists search for _____ life?
   f. One of my principles is that we should never be _____. Honesty is extremely important for our character.

4. What do these sentences mean? Underline the correct alternative.

   I'm worried that they will **disappear** before they pay.

   a. I'm worried that they will appear again before they pay.
   b. I'm worried that they will not appear again before they pay.

   I think you **misunderstood** my instructions. I said you needed to complete it by Thursday, not Tuesday.

   a. I think you didn't understand my instructions correctly. It was Thursday, not Tuesday.
   b. I think you understood my instructions, but decided to complete it on Tuesday instead of Thursday.

LANGUAGE IN USE 1

Unit 5

PLURAL OF NOUNS

1. Read this excerpt from the text on page 46. Focus on the words in bold. Then read the statements and write true (T) or false (F).

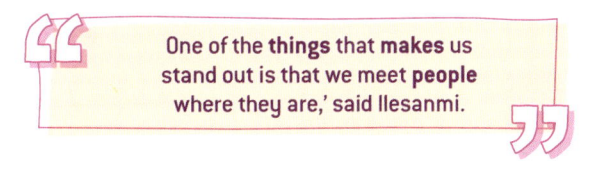

> "One of the **things** that **makes** us stand out is that we meet **people** where they are,' said Ilesanmi.

a. (   ) The letter *s* in English can be used to indicate the plural of a noun and the third person singular of a verb in the simple present.
b. (   ) All plural forms in English are formed with -*s* or -*es*.
c. (   ) Irregular plural forms in English have no rule.
d. (   ) All words in bold in the excerpt indicate a plural form.

2. Look at the table below and complete the rule with the words and letters from the box.

Singular	Plural	Singular	Plural	Singular	Plural
boy	boys	girl	girls	book	books
box	boxes	match	matches	class	classes
brush	brushes	hero	heroes	potato	potatoes
piano	pianos	photo	photos	baby	babies
city	cities	leaf	leaves	life	lives
belief	beliefs	roof	roofs / rooves	man	men
woman	women	child	children	person	people

o	s	ies	y
ves	irregular	es	es
y	f	y	s

Many English nouns form their plural by adding _____ or _____. We usually add _____ to words that end in *s*, *x*, *ch*, *sh* and, sometimes, *o*. However, some words ending in _____ also have their plural form just by the addition of -*s*. When a word ends in a _____ that comes after a consonant, we substitute the _____ for _____ to form the plural. Words ending in a _____ that come after a vowel have their plural form created by adding _____ such as *play*. Some words ending in *f* or in *fe* require you to substitute the *f* or the *fe* for _____. However, other words ending in _____ are made plural by adding *s* only. Some words have _____ plural forms, and need to be memorized.

3. Rewrite these excerpts from the text on page 46 in the plural form. Pay attention to the other changes you need to make.

a. "It's not a gallery, nor a pop-up space, nor the work of an artist who turned an abandoned building into a functioning laundromat."

_____

b. "The type of community engagement fostered by the project isn't about painting a mural and walking away."

_____

4. Look at the new sentences you wrote in activity 3. Then check (✓) the sentences below that are true.

a. (   ) Some words don't have a plural form; they are uncountable nouns.
b. (   ) Don't use indefinite articles with nouns in the plural form. However, it's OK to use the definite article with either the singular or the plural.
c. (   ) Don't make any changes to the pronouns in your sentences.
d. (   ) Adjectives don't have a plural form.

49

EXPAND YOUR READING

1. Look at the pictures below. They show works of art. What do you think they represent?

https://www.metmuseum.org/toah/works-of-art/21.6.73/

Headrest

Date: 19th–20th century
Geography: Zimbabwe
Culture: Shona peoples
Medium: Wood
Dimensions: H. 5 5/8 x W. 6 1/4 x D. 2 1/2 in. (14.3 x 15.9 x 6.4 cm)
Classification: Wood-Furniture
Credit Line: Anonymous Gift, 1986
Accession Number: 1986.484.1

Description
The use of headrests in southern Africa has been traced back to the twelfth-century archaeological site of Mapungubwe, an urban center along the Limpopo River. There, evidence of gold **sheeting** believed to have adorned a long-disintegrated wooden headrest has been recovered.

The designs of such works, created to protect elaborate **coiffures**, reflect a range of regional styles. Among the Shona, headrests were exclusively carved and used by men. Since they also functioned as vehicles of communication with the ancestral **realm**, headrests and other personal articles were frequently **buried** with their owners, evidencing the intimate connection between the object and its owner. In other cases, they were passed along to male descendants.

Extracted from www.metmuseum.org/toah/works-of-art/1986.484.1/. Accessed on September 25, 2018.

Taweret amulet with double head

Period: New Kingdom
Dynasty: Dynasty 18, late–Dynasty 19
Date: ca. 1390–1213 B.C.
Geography: From Egypt
Medium: Blue faience
Dimensions: H. 2 cm (13/16 in.); W. 1.4 cm (9/16 in.); D. 0.4 cm (3/16 in.)
Credit Line: Gift of Lily S. Place, 1921
Accession Number: 21.6.73

Description
Double-headed amulets of the domestic **goddess** Taweret are rare forms and date to the 18th dynasty. Amarna is among the known **findspots** for these, although this particular example is without **provenance**.

Extracted from www.metmuseum.org/toah/works-of-art/21.6.73/. Accessed on November 7, 2018.

2. Check (✔) the correct alternative to complete the sentences below.

   a. The texts are...
   ( ) argumentative.
   ( ) narrative.
   ( ) descriptive.

   b. The purpose of the text "Headrest" is to...
   ( ) give information about and describe a headrest.
   ( ) discuss the pros and cons of headrests.
   ( ) inform readers about the technical features of a headrest.

   c. Both texts were probably taken from...
   ( ) a blog.
   ( ) a news website.
   ( ) a museum website.

3. Now answer the questions that follow.

   a. Which artwork is older?
   _____

   b. Which artwork could only be used by men?
   _____

   c. Why were headrests buried with their owners?
   _____

   d. What is Taweret?
   _____

LANGUAGE IN USE 2

Unit 5

ORDER OF ADJECTIVES

1. Read this excerpt from the text on page 50 again and pay attention to the words in bold.

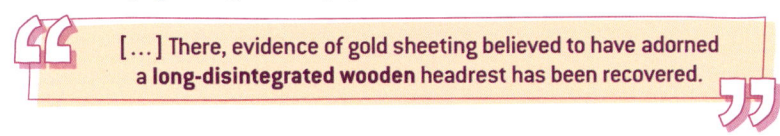

> [...] There, evidence of gold sheeting believed to have adorned a **long-disintegrated wooden** headrest has been recovered.

The words in bold describe and / or add information to the word *headrest*. In English, these words are positioned before the corresponding noun. However, there is a word order to follow.

The most usual sequence of adjectives is as follows (10th = farther from the noun; 1st = closer to the noun):

Order	Relating to	Examples
10th	opinion	interesting, pretty, funny
9th	size	large, small, short
8th	physical quality	organized, slim, messy
7th	shape	square, rectangular, oval
6th	age	old, young, ancient
5th	color	pink, blue, green
4th	origin	Brazilian, American, Australian
3rd	material	wooden, glass, plastic
2nd	type	technological, vegan, self-cleaning
1st	purpose	washing, decorative

2. Rewrite the following sentences. Use the adjectives in parentheses in the correct order.

   a. All the boys were wearing shirts. (clean, flannel, new)

   _____

   b. Jessica's friends fell in love with her classmate. (handsome, Mexican, new)

   _____

   c. He gave his mother a vase. (black, Egyptian, small)

   _____

   d. She sat behind a desk. (big, brown, wooden)

   _____

3. Describe two different objects that you have. Use at least three adjectives to describe each of them.

   _____

   _____

LISTENING COMPREHENSION

1. **You are going to listen to an artist called John McKenna talking about his work. As you listen, number the sentences below in the order the actions are mentioned.**

   ( ) He stopped studying art at college when his father's house was repossessed.
   ( ) Sometimes he thinks he chose the wrong job for his life.
   ( ) He says that it is necessary to have strong motivation to make a living as an artist.
   ( ) He saw a TV program about a sculpture school and knew he wanted to start studying there.
   ( ) He tried studying accountancy, but then he changed to art.
   ( ) He started painting signs and painted 60 signs a day for a supermarket.
   ( ) He was commissioned to sculpt a herd of bronze jersey cows.
   ( ) His mother died when he was very young.

2. **Go to the audio scripts on page 137 and read the personal account again. Then talk to a partner and retell the story.**

   _____
   _____
   _____
   _____
   _____

3. **Read the saying below taken from the audio script. Do you agree with it? Exchange ideas with your classmates.**

   > "What is meant for you doesn't pass by you."

›› EXPAND YOUR HORIZONS ››››

Check (✓) the column that best describes your opinion about each statement. Then discuss your answers with your classmates and teacher, justifying your point of view.

	I agree.	I'm not sure.	I disagree.
a. Art is not meant to transform society, but to represent it.			
b. It is possible to rank different forms of art in terms of their importance.			
c. Traditional art is losing its place and relevance in today's world.			

UNIT 6
Sport is No Longer Just Sport

IN THIS UNIT YOU WILL...
- talk about how sports have become big business;
- learn how to form nouns using suffixes;
- exchange ideas about the inclusion of new sports in the 2020 Olympics;
- make comparisons using the comparative and the superlative forms.

LEAD OFF
- How are the title of this unit and the picture related?
- Has the commercialization of sport changed the behavior of players? How?
- How do sports help nations?

READING

›› BEFORE READING

Work in pairs. List some problems the sports industry faces nowadays.

Bridging and relating to the topic

›› WHILE READING

Scan the text and answer the question: what is it about? Circle at least two elements that justify your answer.

Finding organizational patterns

---

http://politics.uchicago.edu/pages/juliet-macur-seminar-series

THE UNIVERSITY OF CHICAGO INSTITUTE OF POLITICS
HOME ABOUT CAREER DEVELOPMENT CIVIC ENGAGEMENT SPEAKER SERIES FELLOWS PROGRAM MEDIA Facebook Twitter Instagram Youtube

The Power and Politics of Sports: Why Games Aren't Just Games Anymore

Sports used to be simple. Go to games. Play games. Have fun. Be entertained. Now it's so much more. Every level of sports – from your local youth leagues straight up to the pros – has become big business that generates big money and big influence. For good and bad, the sports world is bigger and more powerful than ever, with athletes **wielding** more and more influence over our culture and our politics.

5 RSVP for all of Juliet's seminars here

January 12: The Power of the Athlete

Should athletes keep their focus on the playing field, or do they have a duty to speak out on social issues because so many people look up to them? When Muhammad Ali and Kareem Abdul-Jabbar spoke out about Donald Trump's idea to ban all Muslims from entry into the United States, why did it make an impact? Or, when Russia enacted an anti-gay law before the 2014 Sochi Winter Games, why did so many Olympic athletes refuse to talk about the politics of it, saying sports and politics
10 should **remain** separate? What, exactly, is the duty of the athlete in those situations?

January 19: The FIFA Takedown – Corruption in Soccer and International Sports

One morning last May in Zurich, Swiss law enforcement **raided** a five-star lakeside hotel and arrested some of the world's most powerful officials in worldwide soccer. Those arrests marked the beginning of perhaps the biggest takedown in the history of sports, with FIFA, soccer's global governing body, at the center of it all and United States federal **prosecutors**
15 leading the charge to clean up the sport. How did those FIFA officials reign with so much impunity for so many years? How did the International Olympic Committee allow global soccer to get to this point of such widespread corruption that, by the end of 2015, more than 40 officials in the sport pleaded **guilty** or were arrested for crimes that included receiving bribes and kickbacks? [...]

January 26: Fantasy Football Feud: The Debate over DraftKings & FanDuel

Fantasy-league betting has become a multibillion-dollar industry. But will it soon be extinct? Online daily fantasy sports sites, like DraftKings and FanDuel, are commanding attention now and it's nearly impossible to watch sports on television – or go to
20 a sporting event, for that matter – without seeing their ads. Yet those days might be coming to an end. Those sites and ones like them are at the center of an ongoing, **sizzling** public policy debate that pits whether internet fantasy league gambling is a game of chance or a game of skill. If it's a game of chance, then the government would have to step in to regulate it, or ban it outright. We discuss the future of fantasy leagues and whether they should be legal. Also, does that type of gambling dehumanize the athletes, who feel like disposable pawns in that money-making game? Should fans even care?

February 2: Former US Soccer Captain & Current ESPN Analyst Julie Foudy on Women in Sports

25 The United States women's national soccer team sued FIFA and the Canadian Soccer Association last year, claiming discrimination because the 2015 Women's World Cup had only artificial **turf** fields, instead of grass ones, which is the preferred surface for the game. The team asked: The men's World Cup is played on grass and will be for the foreseeable future, so why do the women have to play on an inferior surface? The women's team backed down from its case, as FIFA basically ran out the clock. Now do these women, whose World Cup-winning final game was the most watched soccer game in United States history, have the power to demand better fields? Or will women in sports always find themselves stuck behind men?

Adapted from http://politics.uchicago.edu/pages/juliet-macur-seminar-series. Accessed on May 25, 2018.

Unit 6

» AFTER READING

Understanding main ideas

1. Check (✓) the issues that are <u>not</u> discussed in the seminars mentioned in the text.
   a. ( ) discrimination   b. ( ) fantasy sports sites   c. ( ) being a sportswriter
   d. ( ) doping   e. ( ) widespread corruption

2. Answer these questions. If necessary, go back to the text. **Understanding details**
   a. What event is considered the starting point of perhaps the biggest dishonor in the history of sports?
   _____
   b. Which online daily fantasy sports sites are mentioned in the text?
   _____
   c. Why did the United States women's national soccer team sue FIFA and the Canadian Soccer Association last year?
   _____
   _____

3. From your view, which seminar brings up the most controversial subject? Explain.

EXPAND YOUR VOCABULARY

1. Find in the text the words that correspond to these definitions. Write them in the blanks.
   a. _____: *noun [uncountable]* when people risk money or possessions on the result of something which is not certain, such as a card game or a horse race → betting
   b. _____: *noun [countable]* informal money that someone pays secretly and dishonestly in return for someone's help
   c. _____: *adjective* too strong to be destroyed or defeated
   d. _____: *noun [countable, uncountable]* something that you have to do because it is morally or legally right
   e. _____: *noun [countable]* someone who is used by a more powerful person or group and has no control of the situation

   Extracted from www.ldoceonline.com. Accessed on June 15, 2018.

2. Read this tweet about sports. Talk to a classmate about whether you agree with it or not.

   > **Vallery Stevens** ✓
   > @Vall_13
   >
   > I realize sport has turned into a business. That's why nowadays I don't get too high or low as far as emotions are concerned. It's a money grab!
   >
   > 4:50 pm – May 25, 2018
   >
   > ♡ 11   💬 21 people are talking about this

55

VOCABULARY IN USE

1. Read a subtitle extracted from another part of the text on page 54.

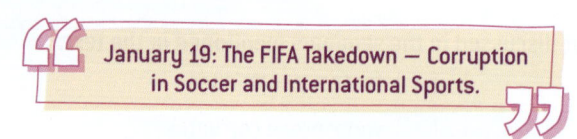

> January 19: The FIFA Takedown — Corruption in Soccer and International Sports.

The suffix -*ion* has changed the verb *corrupt* to the noun *corruption*. Besides -*ion*, the suffixes -*tion*, -*sion*, and -*ation* refer to a state or process; for example, *corruption* is the process of corrupting.

Go back to the text and find other nouns formed by one of these suffixes.

_____

2. Form singular or plural nouns from the verbs in the box to complete the text below.

> compete   participate   populate

Sports in Brazil

Brazilian sports have a very strong heritage in the country. The majority of the _____ often follows and participates in various sports. Sports are considered a large part of the Brazilian culture rather than just being sporting events. Besides soccer being the most popular, Brazil has various other sports that the country is very proud of. They have progressed and earned medals in swimming, sailing, athletics, and judo.

Brazil in the Olympics

Since Brazil has a typically tropical and subtropical climate, it does not usually compete in the Winter Olympics. The country made its first appearance in the Winter Games in 1992, and most recently participated in 2006. Despite their minimal _____ in the Winter Olympics, Brazil has been competing in the Summer Olympics since 1920. Today, they come in at 33rd in the overall ranking of medals in the Summer Olympics.

Top Three Sports in Brazil

Soccer is the most popular sport in Brazil. It is taken very seriously where anything less than a win is, essentially, considered worthless. Volleyball is the second most popular sport in Brazil. Brazil is also the most successful country in this sport. Their men's national volleyball team is currently the champion in the 2 major _____ (Volleyball World Cup and Volleyball World Championship). [...] Brazilian athletes have also greatly succeeded worldwide in beach volleyball.

Adapted from www.thetranslationcompany.com/news/blog/language-news/portuguese/sports-brazil. Accessed on May 25, 2018.

3. Work with a partner. Write about two sports represented below. Use a noun formed by one of the suffixes studied in this section.

| skateboarding |  footvolley |  surfing |  judo |

LANGUAGE IN USE 1

Unit 6

COMPARATIVE ADJECTIVES

1. Read this excerpt from the text on page 54 and underline the correct option to complete the sentences.

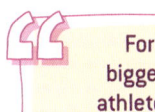

> "For good and bad, the sports world is bigger and more powerful than ever, with athletes wielding more and more influence over our culture and our politics."

   a. The structures used to compare the world of sports are **good and bad / bigger and more powerful**.
   b. The author compares the sports world today to **our culture and politics / the sports world in the past**.
   c. In the author's opinion, the world of sports in the past was **smaller and less powerful than / as big and powerful as** it is now.

2. Complete the table according to what you have studied in activity 1.

	short adjectives	long adjectives
Comparative of superiority	small____ + _____	_____ + powerful + _____
Comparative of inferiority	short or long adjectives	
	_____ + famous + _____	
	_____ + competitive + _____	
Comparative of equality	short or long adjectives	
	____ + big + ____	
	____ + powerful + ____	

3. Read the infographic below and circle the adjectives in the comparative form. Then complete the sentences with the comparative form of the adjectives in parentheses.

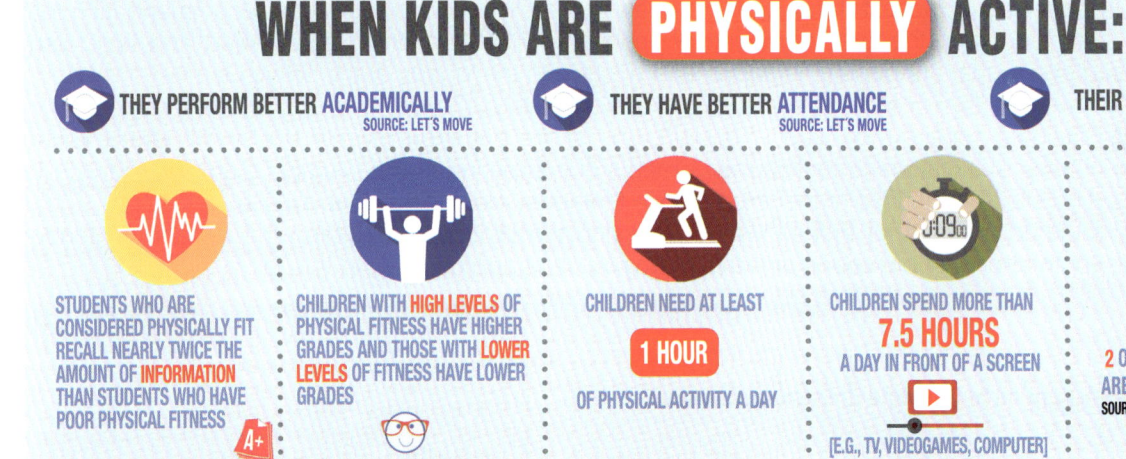

WHEN KIDS ARE PHYSICALLY ACTIVE:

- THEY PERFORM BETTER ACADEMICALLY — SOURCE: LET'S MOVE
- THEY HAVE BETTER ATTENDANCE — SOURCE: LET'S MOVE
- THEIR BEHAVIOR IMPROVES — SOURCE: LET'S MOVE

STUDENTS WHO ARE CONSIDERED PHYSICALLY FIT RECALL NEARLY TWICE THE AMOUNT OF INFORMATION THAN STUDENTS WHO HAVE POOR PHYSICAL FITNESS
SOURCE: THE PUBLIC LIBRARY OF SCIENCE

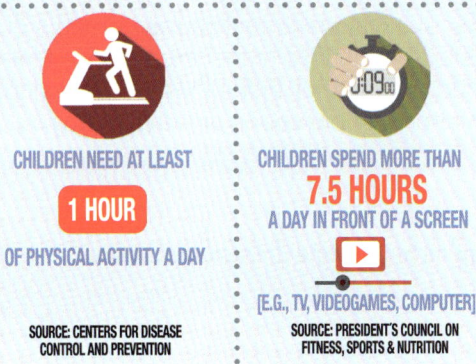

CHILDREN WITH HIGH LEVELS OF PHYSICAL FITNESS HAVE HIGHER GRADES AND THOSE WITH LOWER LEVELS OF FITNESS HAVE LOWER GRADES
SOURCE: THE JOURNAL OF PEDIATRICS

CHILDREN NEED AT LEAST 1 HOUR OF PHYSICAL ACTIVITY A DAY
SOURCE: CENTERS FOR DISEASE CONTROL AND PREVENTION

CHILDREN SPEND MORE THAN 7.5 HOURS A DAY IN FRONT OF A SCREEN [E.G., TV, VIDEOGAMES, COMPUTER]
SOURCE: PRESIDENT'S COUNCIL ON FITNESS, SPORTS & NUTRITION

2 OUT OF 3 KIDS TODAY ARE INACTIVE
SOURCE: LET'S MOVE

Extracted from https://sites.google.com/site/sportsinschoolarevery benficial/counterclaims. Accessed on May 25, 2018.

   a. When kids are not physically active, they have _____ (bad) performance than when they are.
   b. Kids' behavior is _____ (appropriate) when they practice sports.
   c. Students who are physically fit are _____ (good) at recalling information than those who have poor physical fitness.

4. Work in pairs. Ask each other two questions about the infographic using adjectives in the comparative form.

STUDY THIS

Irregular Comparatives

good – better
bad – worse
far – farther / further

little – less
much – more

EXPAND YOUR READING

1. Read the text below and relate it to the one on page 54. In your opinion, how is the addition of five new sports events to the Tokyo Olympics in 2020 associated with the power and politics of sports? Share your opinion with your classmates.

---

https://www.olympic.org/news/ioc-approves-five-new-sports-for-olympic-games-tokyo-2020

IOC APPROVES FIVE NEW SPORTS FOR OLYMPIC GAMES TOKYO 2020

Updated 1658 GMT (0058 HKT) August 4, 2016

THE INTERNATIONAL OLYMPIC COMMITTEE (IOC) TODAY AGREED TO ADD BASEBALL/SOFTBALL, KARATE, SKATEBOARDING, SPORTS CLIMBING AND SURFING TO THE SPORTS PROGRAM FOR THE OLYMPIC GAMES TOKYO 2020.

The decision by the 129th IOC Session in Rio de Janeiro was the most comprehensive evolution of the Olympic program in modern history. Plans call for **staging** the skateboarding and sports climbing events in temporary **venues** installed in urban settings, marking a historic step in bringing the Games to young people and reflecting the trend of urbanization of sport.

5 The Organizing Committee for the Tokyo 2020 Games proposed the five new sports in response to the new flexibility provided by Olympic Agenda 2020.

[…]

Tokyo 2020, the first Organizing Committee able to take advantage of the change, submitted its proposal for the five new sports to the IOC in September 2015.

10 IOC President Thomas Bach said, "We want to take sport to the **youth**. With the many options that young people have, we cannot expect any more that they will come automatically to us. We have to go to them. Tokyo 2020's balanced proposal **fulfills** all of the goals of the Olympic Agenda 2020 recommendation that allowed it. Taken together, the five sports are an innovative combination of established and emerging, youth-focused events that are popular in Japan and will add to the legacy of the Tokyo Games."

15 […]

Tokyo 2020 President Yoshiro Mori said, "The inclusion of the package of new sports will **afford** young athletes the chance of a lifetime to realize their dreams of competing in the Olympic Games – the world's greatest sporting stage – and inspire them to achieve their best, both in sport and in life."

The IOC considered a variety of factors when assessing the proposal, including the impact on gender
20 equality, the youth appeal of the sports and the legacy value of adding them to the Tokyo Games.

Adapted from www.olympic.org/news/ioc-approves-five-new-sports-for-olympic-games-tokyo-2020. Accessed on July 25, 2018.

---

2. Check (✓) the correct option to complete the sentences below.

a. The text is…
- ( ) an interview.
- ( ) a scientific article.
- ( ) a news report.

b. The purpose of the text is to…
- ( ) inform readers about the inclusion of new sports in the 2020 Tokyo Olympic Games.
- ( ) discuss sports as social tools to be implemented in Tokyo in 2020.
- ( ) offer a critical perspective on urban sports in Tokyo in a humorous way.

c. The text deals with…
- ( ) a sequence of events about a famous person's life.
- ( ) a contemporary topic that interests a vast audience.
- ( ) a known fact described in the first person singular.

d. The number of sports being introduced in the 2020 Tokyo Olympic Games is…
- ( ) four.
- ( ) five.
- ( ) seven.

LANGUAGE IN USE 2

Unit 6

SUPERLATIVE ADJECTIVES

1. Below you will find some extracts from the news report on page 58. Read them and match the sentence halves to form meaningful statements about superlatives.

> "The decision by the 129th IOC Session in Rio de Janeiro was **the most comprehensive** evolution of the Olympic program in modern history [...]"

> "[...] the chance of a lifetime to realize their dreams of competing in the Olympic Games – the world's **greatest** sporting stage – and inspire them to achieve their **best**, both in sport and in life."

a. In the first extract, *the evolution* is compared to...
b. In the second extract, *the Olympic Games* are compared to...
c. The word *best* is...

( ) the superlative form of the adjective *good*.
( ) all the evolutions of the Olympics in modern history.
( ) all the sporting stages.

2. Now based on activity 1, complete the following statements.

a. To form the superlative of most long adjectives, we use _____ before them.

b. To form the superlative of most short adjectives, we add _____ to them.

c. In superlatives, it is common to use the definite article _____ before adjectives.

d. Some adjectives such as *good* and *bad*, for example, have irregular forms in their superlatives. Those are _____ and *the worst*, respectively.

STUDY THIS

Irregular Superlatives

good – best	little – least	far – farthest / furthest
bad – worst	much – most	

3. Use the superlative form of the adjectives from the box to complete the quotes below.

> bad   great   hard   high

a. "I always felt that my _____ asset was not my physical ability, it was my mental ability." – Caitlyn Jenner

b. "Make sure your _____ enemy doesn't live between your own two ears." – Laird Hamilton

c. "You are never really playing an opponent. You are playing yourself, your own _____ standards, and when you reach your limits, that is real joy." – Arthur Ashe

d. "The _____ skill to acquire in this sport is the one where you compete all out, give it all you have, and you are still getting beat no matter what you do. When you have the killer instinct to fight through that, it is very special." – Eddie Reese

Extracted from www.keepinspiring.me/100-most-inspirational-sports-quotes-of-all-time. Accessed on May 28, 2018.

4. Underline a superlative structure in the text fragment below. Then rewrite the whole sentence using a synonym.

Currently, there are an estimated 30 million people worldwide who skate at least once a week.

[...]
Chris Cole is a professional American skateboarder who is excited at the possible prospect of competing at the Olympic Games.
The 32-year-old is one of the most recognizable stars in the skateboarding community, winning numerous gold medals at the X-Games – an annual event for extreme sports.
[...]

Adapted from www.bbc.com/sport/olympics/27372110. Accessed on May 28, 2018.

_____
_____
_____

59

LISTENING COMPREHENSION

1. Read the infographic below and answer: Who are millennials? In your opinion, do they influence the sports industry? Justify your answer.

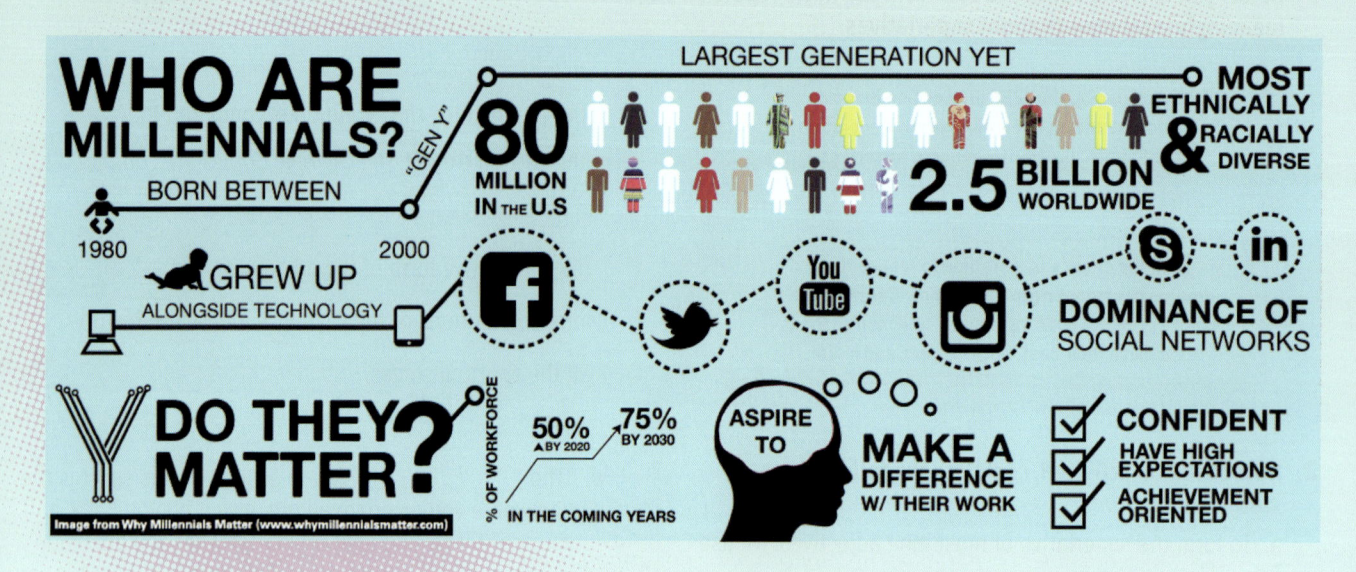

WHO ARE MILLENNIALS? "GEN Y"
BORN BETWEEN 1980 – 2000
GREW UP ALONGSIDE TECHNOLOGY

LARGEST GENERATION YET
80 MILLION IN THE U.S
2.5 BILLION WORLDWIDE
MOST ETHNICALLY & RACIALLY DIVERSE

DOMINANCE OF SOCIAL NETWORKS

DO THEY MATTER?
50% OF WORKFORCE BY 2020
75% BY 2030
% IN THE COMING YEARS

ASPIRE TO MAKE A DIFFERENCE W/ THEIR WORK

CONFIDENT
HAVE HIGH EXPECTATIONS
ACHIEVEMENT ORIENTED

Image from Why Millennials Matter (www.whymillennialsmatter.com)

Extracted from http://whymillennialsmatter.com. Accessed on May 27, 2018.

2. Listen to the conclusions of a study comparing the involvement in sports by millennials and non-millennials. Then complete the blanks with numbers.

   08

   a. Non-millennials spend _____% of their media time watching sports on television.

   b. They spend _____% of that time on online TV.

   c. Millennials spend _____% of their time watching sports on television.

   d. They spend _____% of that time on online TV.

   e. The survey was conducted with more than _____ people.

   f. _____% of millennial sports fans say that they prefer e-sports to traditional sports.

   g. _____% of non-millennial sports fans say that they prefer e-sports to traditional sports.

3. Why do you think millenials are less involved in traditional sports than previous generations? Exchange ideas with your classmates.

»EXPAND YOUR HORIZONS »»»

Check (✔) the column that best describes your opinion about each statement. Then discuss your answers with your classmates and teacher, justifying your point of view.

	I agree.	I'm not sure.	I disagree.
a. Commercialization of sports is definitely inevitable because it empowers players financially and keeps professional sports highly qualified and entertaining.			
b. As sports have become more professional and politicized in the past years, corrupting effects have also emerged.			
c. The inclusion of new sports in the Olympics certainly favors the younger generation of athletes.			

REVIEW 3

Unit 5 and 6

1. Read the text and check (✓) the picture that corresponds to the type of art it describes. *Relating to the topic*

   a ( )   b ( )

What is Installation Art? | History and Top Art Installations Since 2013

By My Modern Met Team on April 15, 2018

Like most movements that make up modern and contemporary **art**, installation art exhibits an interest in innovating. **Though** similar to sculpture and related to a range of recent artistic **genres**, the immersive practice offers a unique way to experience art. In order to **grasp** the significance of such a movement, it is important to understand what makes it so special, from its distinctive qualities to its artistic influences.

[…]

What is Installation Art?

Installation art is a modern movement characterized by immersive, larger-than-life **works of art**. Usually, installation artists create these pieces for specific locations, enabling them to **expertly** transform any space into a customized, interactive **environment**.

[…]

A key attribute of installation art is its ability to physically interact with viewers. While all artistic mediums have the ability to engage individuals, most do not completely immerse them in interactive experiences.

In addition to facilitating dialogues between observers and works of art, this unique characteristic invites individuals to view art from new and different **perspectives**—literally!

[…]

PERFORMANCE ART

While performance art—a practice performed before an audience—may seem dissimilar to installation, a form of fine art, the two movements are linked by a key characteristic: a creative and conceptual **use** of space. In both cases, artists find innovative and inventive **ways** to reinterpret and reimagine everyday environments.

Extracted from www.mymodernmet.com/what-is-installation-art-history-artists. Accessed on June 15, 2018.

2. Underline the statement that is <u>not</u> true according to the text. *Understanding details*

   a. Installation art provides opportunities for observers to really interact with art.
   b. Installation art is modern, innovative, and often collaborative as well.
   c. Performance and installation arts are completely disassociated movements.
   d. Communication between spectators and works of art is easier with installations.
   e. Artistis are innovative when they reinterpret everyday environments.

3. Refer back to the text on page 61 and find the adjectives used to qualify the nouns in bold.

   a. _____ art
   b. _____ genres
   c. _____ works of art
   d. _____ environment
   e. _____ perspectives
   f. _____ use
   g. _____ ways

4. Which nouns in the text follow the same plural spelling rule shown in *qualities* in "from its distinctive *qualities* to its artistic influences"?

   a. (   ) way, ability
   b. (   ) ability, history
   c. (   ) history, way
   d. (   ) exhibit, history

5. Read some headlines related to sports news. Then fill in the blanks with the adjectives from the box in the comparative or superlative form.

   > fast   good   bad   old

   a. **Kilian Jornet: inside the mind of the world's _____ mountain runner**
   Kilian Jornet, 29, is widely considered the world's best ultra-distance and mountain runner. Last month, he conquered Mount Everest twice in one week without using supplemental oxygen or fixed ropes. [...]
   Extracted from www.theguardian.com. Accessed on November 9, 2018.

   b. **D-day veteran becomes world's _____ skydiver at 101 and 38 days**
   Verdun Hayes breaks record by completing tandem skydive with three generations of his family in Devon
   Extracted from www.theguardian.com. Accessed on November 9, 2018.

   c. **French sailor François Gabart makes _____ solo circumnavigation**
   Journey around world took 42 days and 16 hours – six days faster than previous record
   Extracted from www.theguardian.com. Accessed on November 9, 2018.

   d. **The decline of competitive sports days is a tragedy – but a lack of exercise is even _____**
   Competitive sports are good – and fun
   Extracted from www.telegraph.co.uk. Accessed on November 9, 2018.

6. Use the cues to write affirmative or negative sentences in the comparative form.

   a. Verdun Hayes / be / much old / Kilian Jornet
   _____

   b. The previous fastest solo circumnavigation / be / six days / long / François Gabart's solo circumnavigation
   _____

   c. Mountain runners / be usually / well equipped / Kilian Jornet
   _____

   d. People / be / competitive / in the past / they / be / now
   _____

UNIT 7

Globish: Fad or Fact?

▶ IN THIS UNIT YOU WILL…

- understand the concept of *Globish*;
- discuss the importance of speaking English nowadays;
- distinguish the difference between possessive adjectives and possessive pronouns;
- learn how to use *'s* to indicate possession.

LEAD OFF

> "The size of your world is proportional to the number of languages you speak." Do you agree with this statement?
> How important is the English language in today's world?
> What if English became the only language spoken in the world?

READING

BEFORE READING

How much do you know about Globish? Check (✓) the statements that you think are true. Then read the text and check your answers. *Activating previous knowledge*

a. ( ) Globish is a sophisticated version of English used by native speakers.
b. ( ) The word *Globish* is a blend of the words *Globe* and *English*.
c. ( ) Globish is an international auxiliary language used by non-native speakers.

WHILE READING

Read part of an article about the Globish revolution. According to the writer, is it easier or harder to communicate with business people using Globish? *Scanning*

So, what's this Globish revolution?

I say tomato... you say red, round fruit. Increasingly, people across the world use some sort of English, but it is not the Queen's. Robert McCrum, Observer Literary Editor, reports on why Globish - English-lite - is becoming the universal language of the **boardroom**, the net and politics

Jean-Paul Nerriere is the kind of high-flying Frenchman at which the Grandes Ecoles excel: cosmopolitan, **witty**, voluble and insatiably
5 curious about the world around him. Formerly a naval commander, then a businessman, he is the proud holder of the Legion d'Honneur. In his blue blazer and **cravat**, twinkly Nerriere cuts a **dashing** figure, seems much younger than his 65 years
10 and occupies a surprising place in contemporary European culture.

In scenes reminiscent of Lost in Translation, Nerriere noted that his conversation with the Japanese and Koreans was 'much easier and more efficient than what could be observed
15 between them and the British and American (IBM) employees who came with me'. A thoughtful man, with a fascination for the exploits of Nelson, he noted that this observation of non-Anglophone English communication applied to
20 'all non-English-speaking countries'.

Then Nerriere came to his radical, perhaps revolutionary, conclusion: 'The language non-Anglophones spoke together,' he says, 'was not English, but something vaguely like it.'
25 In this language, he noted, 'we were better off than genuine Anglophones'. This language, he decided, 'was the worldwide dialect of the third millennium'. In a moment of pure inspiration he called it 'Globish' (pronounced 'globe-ish').

30 Globish is not '**pidgin**' or 'broken' English but it is highly simplified and unidiomatic. Nerriere observes that in Globish you could never say, 'This **erstwhile** buddy of yours is a weird duck who will probably **put the kibosh on** all our good
35 **deeds**.' That might make sense on Acacia Avenue but it will not play in Buenos Aires or Zurich. In Globish you would express this as: 'Your old friend is too strange. He would ruin all our efforts.' Globish, says Nerriere, is
40 'decaffeinated English, or English-lite'.

[...]

Nerriere himself is sometimes described as a remarkable man whose ambition is to promote global understanding between nationalities. He speaks passionately about his hopes for
45 Globish as 'an official language that would facilitate the life of everyone and put everyone on a par'. He hopes that 'some day it will be accepted as a viable alternative by the European Union or the United Nations'.

[...]

Extracted from www.theguardian.com/theobserver/2006/dec/03/features.review37. Accessed on August 08, 2018.

›› AFTER READING

Scan the text and find the information below. *Scanning*

a. What is this sort of English becoming a universal language called?
___

b. What is Jean-Paul Nerriere's nationality?
___

c. Was it easier for Jean-Paul Nerriere or the British and Americans with him to communicate with the Japanese and Koreans?
___

d. What was Nerriere's conclusion?
___

e. What characteristics does the writer give to Globish?
___

f. How does he simplify the statement: 'This erstwhile buddy of yours is a weird duck who will probably put the kibosh on all our good deeds.'
___

EXPAND YOUR VOCABULARY

1. **Choose the correct synonym for each word in bold. If necessary, refer back to the text.**

   a. "Jean-Paul Nerriere is the kind of **high-flying** Frenchman [...]"
      - ( ) failed
      - ( ) successful

   b. "[...] **twinkly** Nerriere cuts a dashing figure, seems much younger than his 65 years and occupies a surprising place in contemporary European culture."
      - ( ) friendly
      - ( ) unfriendly

   c. "We were **better off** than genuine Anglophones."
      - ( ) more fortunate
      - ( ) more helpless

   d. "Nerriere himself is sometimes described as a **remarkable** man [...]"
      - ( ) extremely intelligent
      - ( ) positively surprising

   e. "[...] Globish as 'an official language that would facilitate the life of everyone and put everyone **on a par**'."
      - ( ) at different levels
      - ( ) at the same level

2. What do you think the author meant by "Globish [...] is <u>decaffeinated</u> English, or <u>English-lite</u>"?
___

VOCABULARY IN USE

1. **Reread this excerpt from the text on page 64 and choose the best option to complete the sentences.**

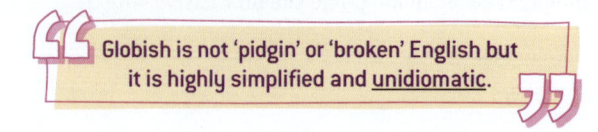

   > Globish is not 'pidgin' or 'broken' English but it is highly simplified and <u>unidiomatic</u>.

   a. By employing the underlined expression, the author means that people who speak Globish **use** / **do not use** idioms in their speech.

   b. Idioms are combinations of words whose meaning is **difficult** / **easy** to guess from the meaning of each individual word.

2. **The idioms in bold in the sentences below are related to body parts. Read the sentences and infer the meaning of the idioms. Then match the columns.**

   a. Susan always **has butterflies in her stomach** before she speaks in public.

   b. Jack is **the apple of his father's eye**.

   c. I was going to buy that new cell phone, but it costs **an arm and a leg**!

   (   ) loved and cherished by someone
   (   ) becomes nervous
   (   ) a lot of money

3. **Complete the sentences below with the idioms from the box. Make all the necessary changes.**

   > put your foot in your mouth   know your onions   apples and oranges   a piece of cake   cup of tea
   > have a finger in every pie   cold feet   give someone the cold shoulder   know something by heart

   a. I don't need you to remind me the lyrics of that song. I _____.
   b. That was probably the easiest game we've ever played! It was _____!
   c. I didn't mean to offend you, really! I guess I just _____.
   d. In all honesty, pop music is not my _____. I prefer rock.
   e. If you have any questions about language, you can ask James. He really _____.
   f. Mary doesn't like focusing on one thing only! She _____.
   g. You can't really compare riding a bike to traveling by plane. It's like _____! Two completely different things!
   h. I saw Judy at the party, but she _____. I don't know why she ignored me like that.
   i. I thought I'd be OK with it, but now I'm not sure I want to travel. I'm getting _____ about this trip.

4. **Work with a partner. Think of three sentences with any idiom from the previous activity. Two sentences have to be true about you, and one has to be false. Guess which is your partner's false sentence.**

   _____
   _____
   _____
   _____

LANGUAGE IN USE 1

Unit 7

THE 'S FOR POSSESSION

1. The excerpt below is from the reading text on page 64. Circle the possessive with 's.

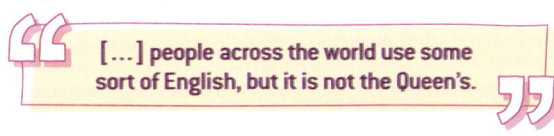

> [...] people across the world use some sort of English, but it is not the Queen's.

2. Read the sentences below, paying close attention to the 's. Then write P for the ones that refer to a possessive and B for the ones that refer to the verb *be*.

a. ( ) Will's here because learning a foreign language is important for our future.

b. ( ) That woman's language is very different from ours. Is it Japanese?

c. ( ) What's the text about?

d. ( ) Kelly's Spanish teacher wants to retire next year.

3. Now analyze the structures in bold in the sentences below and complete the rules with the words from the box.

> a. This is **that blond girl's old doll**.
> b. If you'd like to play with **the children's toys**, you should ask them for permission.
> c. You cannot get those books. They are **our teachers' books**.
> d. Jack and Jill are siblings. **Jack and Jill's parents** are at home now.
> e. **John's and Mary's cars** were stolen on the same day!

| plural | after | each one | 's | ' | irregular | one object |

a. We add _____ to nouns in the singular form to express possession.

b. The possessed item always comes _____ the person who has the possession.

c. We add only _____ when the possession refers to a regular noun in the _____ form.

d. If the noun has an _____ plural form, we need to use 's to form the possessive.

e. If there is only _____ that belongs to two or more people, we add 's only after the last person.

f. If there are two different objects that belong to two or more different people, we use the 's after _____ of the people.

4. Rewrite the sentences below using 's or '.

a. The sister of my uncle speaks six different languages.
_____

b. The mother of Susan and Michael is a very nice lady who was born overseas.
_____

c. This car belongs to those women.
_____

d. These T-shirts belong to the students.
_____

5. Now rewrite these sentences with the verbs given also expressing possession.

a. This is my sister's computer. (belongs)
_____

b. That is Jack's car. (owns)
_____

c. This is Lucas's bike. (has)
_____

67

EXPAND YOUR READING

1. Read the text and answer: Is it a book summary or a book review?

The Future of English?

This book is about the English language in the 21st century: about who will speak it and for what **purposes**. It is a practical briefing document, written for educators, politicians, managers – any decision maker or planning team with a professional interest in the development of English worldwide.

The book explores the possible long-term impact on the English language from developments in communications technology, growing economic globalization and major demographic **shifts** at the end of the twentieth century and **beyond**. It uses existing linguistic research as a basis for examining new trends in globalization, popular culture, and economic development to see how these affect the future use of English.

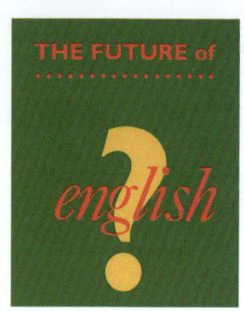

'The Future of English?' **takes stock of** the present position of English in the world and asks **whether** we can expect its status to remain unchanged during the coming decades of unprecedented social and economic global change. The book concludes that the future is more complex and less predictable than has usually been assumed.

First published in 1997, the book was commissioned by the British Council and was intended to stimulate constructive debate about the future status of English at that time.

The book is divided into five main sections:
Section 1 – How English reached its position
Section 2 – Techniques of **forecasting** and identifying patterns of linguistic change
Section 3 – Significant global social and economic trends
Section 4 – The impact of such trends on language and communication
Section 5 – A summary of the impact for the English language

About the author
David Graddol is a British applied linguist, well known as a writer, **broadcaster**, **researcher**, and consultant on issues relating to global English.

Adapted from https://englishagenda.britishcouncil.org/continuing-professional-development/cpd-managers/future-english. Accessed on July 23, 2018.
Reproduced with kind permission of the British Council.

2. Identify the incorrect information in the sentences below. Then rewrite them with the correct information.

a. The book is recommended for students who are learning English.

b. The book examines new trends in education to see how they affect the future use of English.

c. The author did not have the intention of stimulating constructive debate about the future status of English when it was first published.

LANGUAGE IN USE 2

Unit 7

POSSESSIVE PRONOUNS

1. Based on the comic strip complete the examples.

> YOURS substitutes for **your weird dream**.
> MINE substitutes for **my weird dream**.
> THEIRS substitutes for **their weird dream**.

In English, we use a **possessive pronoun** when we replace both the noun and the possessive adjective or the 's for one single pronoun. For example:

> My car → _____
> Susan's books → _____

Remember that it is important for your interlocutor to know what you are talking about when you use only a pronoun. For example:

That is his dog, and this is **mine**. (my dog)

2. Possessive pronouns are used in reference to the possessor and, as such, are closely linked to subject pronouns. It's important not to confuse them with possessive adjectives. Complete the table below to visualize the differences between them.

Subject pronoun	Possessive adjective	Possessive pronoun
I	my	
You	your	
He	his	
She	her	
It	its	
We	our	
They	their	

3. Complete the sentences below with possessive adjectives or possessive pronouns.

a. I have _____ books, and William has _____.

b. David doesn't want to talk to _____ parents, but you can talk to _____.

c. We are going to wait for _____ friends. Donna and Albert are going to wait for _____.

d. Are you asking them to share _____ secrets without sharing _____ first?

e. Jane and Sean are coming over to pick up _____ cat, Yaros… Yarosv… What is _____ name again?

f. This is not Matthew's car, it's Anna's. _____ is older than Matthew's.

69

LISTENING COMPREHENSION

1. Will English always be the global language? What has made it the global language today? Discuss your thoughts with a classmate.

2. You will hear part of a talk given by Dr. David Crystal, one of the most renowned linguists of our times. He is answering the question, "Will English always be the global language?". Check (✓) the sentences below that correspond with David Crystal's views.

   09

   a. ( ) It was easy to have predicted that Latin was no longer going to be spoken by the vast majority of the globe.
   b. ( ) We can't be sure if English will be the dominant language in 100 years' time.
   c. ( ) The future of language and the future of society are connected.
   d. ( ) There are many reasons why a language becomes global.
   e. ( ) People want to speak a foreign language because of power.
   f. ( ) Among the reasons why English became global, we can mention the Industrial Revolution.
   g. ( ) The Internet is still monolingual.
   h. ( ) It is very difficult to imagine a scenario in which English won't be the global language.
   i. ( ) Spanish is the fastest-growing language in the world.
   j. ( ) English will retain the title of global language for the short-term future.

   Extracted from www.youtube.com/watch?v=5Kvs8SxN8mc. Accessed on June 29, 2018.

3. How similar or how different were his answers from yours in activity 1? Write down the two most important things that David Crystal mentioned in his talk and compare them with a classmate.

   _____
   _____

≫ EXPAND YOUR HORIZONS ≫≫≫

Check (✓) the column that best describes your opinion about each statement below. Then discuss your answers with your classmates and teacher, justifying your point of view.

	I agree.	I'm not sure.	I disagree.
a. If we speak Globish, we have access to a broader range of information, connections, and opportunities.			
b. It is possible that one day English will no longer be one of the world's most used languages.			
c. English should not be the leading language as it is not the most popular language.			

UNIT 8
Hit the Road

▶ IN THIS UNIT YOU WILL...
- talk about the means of transportation used for long-distance travels;
- exchange ideas about traveling smart and packing light;
- refer to past actions with *used to*;
- use the modal verb *must*.

LEAD OFF

- What does the picture represent? How is it related to the title of this unit?
- Have you ever heard the expression *travel smart*? What do you think it means?
- What are the means of transportation people often use for short trips? What about long trips?

READING

BEFORE READING — Predicting the theme and the literary genre

Look at the book cover below and read the synopsis that follows. What do you think the book is about? And what genre of book is it?

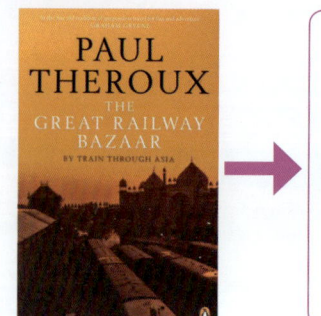

> Paul Theroux is a vocal **proponent** of rail travel over air travel, which he **likens** to traveling by submarine for all that goes unseen and not experienced by its adherents. *The Great Railway Bazaar*, his 1975 account of a four-month railroad journey through Europe and Asia begins, "I **sought** trains, I found passengers." It is certainly the individuals that Theroux meets along the way, rather than the cities, buildings, or sites of touristic import, to which he devotes his most generous descriptions.
>
> Adapted from THEROUX, Paul. The Great Railway Bazaar. PLACE: Penguin, YEAR, p. 2.

WHILE READING

Scan the text. Do you expect it to be narrative or argumentative? Mention the characteristics that support your answer.

Recognizing textual types

Chapter Two THE DIRECT-ORIENT EXPRESS

Duffill had put on a pair of glasses, wire-framed and with enough Scotch tape on the lenses to prevent his seeing the Blue **Mosque**. He assembled his parcels and, **grunting**, produced a suitcase, bound with a selection of leather and canvas belts as an added guarantee against it **bursting** open. A few cars down we met again to read the sign on the side of the wagon-lit: direct-orient and its itinerary, PARIS – LAUSANNE –
5 MILANO – TRIESTE – ZAGREB – BEOGRAD – SOFIYA – ISTANBUL. We stood there, staring at this sign; Duffill worked his glasses like binoculars. Finally he said, 'I took this train in nineteen twenty-nine.'
   It seemed to call for a reply, but by the time a reply occurred to me ('Judging from its condition, it was probably this very train!') Duffill had gathered up his parcels and his **strapped** suitcase and moved down the platform. It was a great train in 1929, and it goes without saying that the Orient Express is the most famous train
10 in the world. Like the Trans-Siberian, it links Europe with Asia, which **accounts** for some of its romance. But it has also been hallowed by fiction: **restless** Lady Chatterley took it; so did Hercule Poirot and James Bond; […]
   After several minutes the rest of the passengers went into their compartments – from my own I heard the smashing of paper parcels being stuffed into corners. This left the drinker, whom I had started to think of as the Captain, and me alone in the passage. He looked my way and said, 'Istanbul?'
15 'Yes.'
   'Have a drink.'
   […]
   His name was Molesworth, but he said it so distinctly that the first time I heard it I thought it was a **double-barreled** name. There was something military in his posture and the promptness of his speech, and at the same time this **flair** could have been an actor's. […]
20 'I'm an actors' agent,' he said. 'I've got my own firm in London. It's a smallish firm, but we do all right. We always have more than we can handle.'
   'Any actors I might know?'
   He named several famous actors.
   I said, 'I thought you might be army.'
25 '*Did* you?' He said that he had been in the Indian army – Poona, Simla, Madras – and his duties there were of a theatrical nature, organizing shows for the troops. […]
   We talked about Indian trains. Molesworth said they were magnificent. 'They have showers, and there's always a little man who brings you what you need. At mealtime they telegraph ahead to the next station for hampers. Oh, you'll like it.'
30 Duffill put his head out the door and said, 'I think I'll go to bed now.'
   'He's your **chap**, is he?' said Molesworth. He surveyed the car. 'This train isn't what it was. Pity. It used to be one of the best, a *train de luxe* – royalty took it. Now, I'm not sure about this, but I don't think we have a dining car, which is going to be a terrible bore if it's true. Have you got a **hamper**?'
   I said I hadn't, though I had been advised to bring one.
35 'That was good advice,' Molesworth said. 'I don't have a hamper myself, but then I don't eat much. I like the *thought* of food, but I much prefer drinking. How do you like your Chablis? Will you have more?' He inserted his eyeglass and found the bottle and, **pouring**, said, 'These French wines take an awful lot of **beating**.'

Adapted from THEROUX, Paul. **The Great Railway Bazaar.** Penguin, General UK, 2008, p. 14, 16, and 17.

Unit 8

›› AFTER READING

1. Check (✓) the statement that best summarizes the excerpt you have just read. `Understanding main ideas`
   a. ( ) The writer is recounting the beginning of his friend's journey on a modern streetcar in Istanbul.
   b. ( ) The narrator is detailing the start of his travel on the Direct-Orient Express to Istanbul.
   c. ( ) Duffill is telling the story about his trip from London to Istanbul on the Direct-Orient Express.

2. Whose voices are those in the text? `Recognizing the voices in a text`
   _____
   _____

3. Decide if the sentences are true (T) or false (F). `Understanding details`
   a. ( ) In Molesworth's opinion, the Orient Express is better off these days than it was in the past.
   b. ( ) Duffill wasn't carrying any luggage.
   c. ( ) The Orient Express taken by the narrator ran between Paris and Istanbul.
   d. ( ) The narrator brought a hamper along because a friend had advised him to do so.
   e. ( ) Although he was not an actor, Molesworth's elegant style made him look like one.

EXPAND YOUR VOCABULARY

1. Match the words in bold with their meanings.
   a. "He assembled his **parcels** and, grunting, produced a suitcase, [...]"
   b. "He inserted his eyeglass and found the bottle and, **pouring**, said, [...]"
   c. "After several minutes the rest of the passengers went into their **compartments** [...]"
   d. "Duffill had gathered up his parcels and his strapped suitcase and moved down the **platform**."
   e. "But it has also been **hallowed** by fiction: [...]"
   f. "It's a **smallish** firm, but we do all right."

   ( ) separate areas into which a plane, ship, or train is divided
   ( ) objects that have been wrapped in paper or put in a special envelope
   ( ) respected or greatly admired
   ( ) an adjective to describe something fairly small
   ( ) making a liquid or other substance flow out of or into a container by holding it at an angle
   ( ) the raised place beside a railway track where you get on and off a train in a station

   Adapted from www.ldoceonline.com. Accessed on June 20, 2018.

2. What are the most common means of transportation for long distances? What means of transportation do you use on long-distance trips? How can you compare ship to air travel in terms of speed, comfort, and luggage capacity? Exchange ideas with a classmate.

VOCABULARY IN USE

1. In the extract "He assembled his parcels and, grunting, produced a suitcase, bound with a selection of leather and canvas belts as an added guarantee against it bursting open.", which words refer to travel packing or bag types?

2. Below you will find other travel packing or bag types. Work in pairs to match them with their corresponding pictures.
   - **a.** suitcase
   - **b.** duffel bag
   - **c.** backpack
   - **d.** toiletry bag
   - **e.** messenger bag
   - **f.** laptop case
   - **g.** rolling suitcase
   - **h.** garment bag

   ( )   ( )   ( )   ( )

   ( )   ( )   ( )   ( )

3. Insert the words from the box in the correct mind map. Then come up with one more item to fit each category.

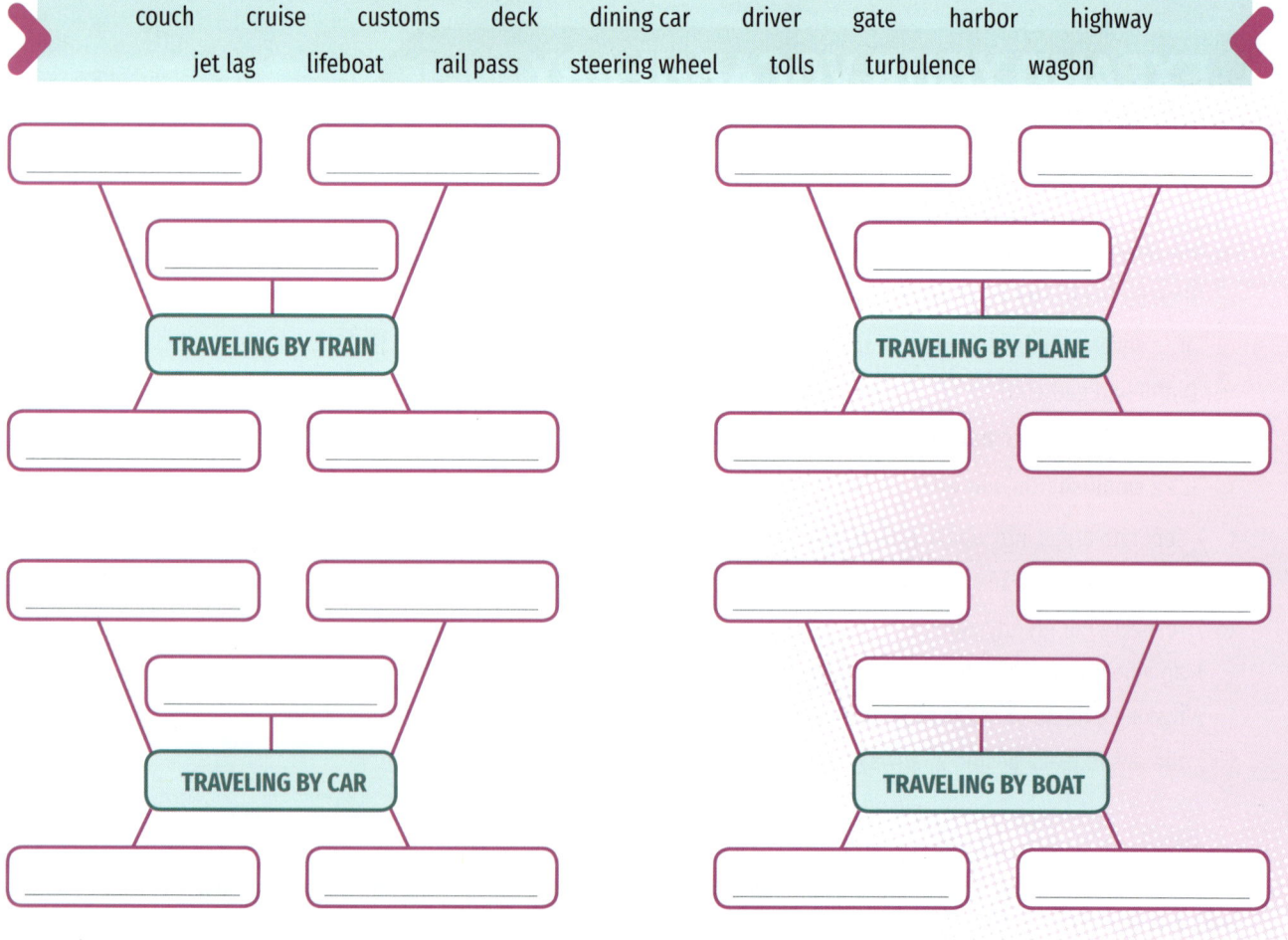

   | couch | cruise | customs | deck | dining car | driver | gate | harbor | highway |
   | jet lag | lifeboat | rail pass | steering wheel | tolls | turbulence | wagon |

   TRAVELING BY TRAIN

   TRAVELING BY PLANE

   TRAVELING BY CAR

   TRAVELING BY BOAT

4. Work with a partner. Describe your ideal type of travel using some words from the previous activities.

LANGUAGE IN USE 1

Unit 8

USED TO

1. The excerpt below was extracted from the text on page 72. Read it, pay special attention to the part in bold, and check (✓) the correct statement about it.

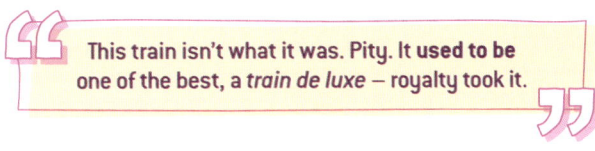

> "This train isn't what it was. Pity. It **used to be one of the best**, a *train de luxe* – royalty took it."

( ) It refers to a regular past state or habit that is finished now.
( ) It refers to a regular past state or habit that is still happening now.

2. Read the text below and answer the questions accordingly.

How have our travel habits changed over the past 50 years?

October 21, 2015 9:58 A.M. EDT

We tend to assume that travel today is fundamentally different from what it was half a century ago. We have easier access to faster forms of transport, and we expect to be able to move quickly and easily whenever we **wish**. But a recent overview of travel behavior in England—celebrating 50 years of data from the National Travel Survey (NTS)—shows that while some things have certainly changed, much remains the same.

According to the authors of the report, the most **striking** change to our travel habits is that "we are traveling further but not more often". In other words, though the individual trips we take are longer in terms of distance, the number of times we travel has **remained** much the same over the past 50 years. What's more, there has been little change in the total time spent traveling, due to faster travel speeds. And the purposes of our trips have changed only slightly: the biggest change has been an increase in the number of journeys we take to escort others.

[…]

Adapted from www.theconversation.com/how-have-our-travel-habits-changed-over-the-past-50-years-49029. Accessed on June 10, 2018.

a. Do we have easy access to faster forms of transport nowadays?
_____

b. **Did** we **use to** have such an easy access to those quicker means of travel 50 years ago?
_____

c. According to the report of travel behavior in England, are they traveling more often these days?
_____

d. How far **did** they **use to** travel 50 years ago?
_____

3. Now reread the extract in activity 1 and the questions and answers in activity 2 to complete the sentences about *used to*.

a. We use _____ followed by the main verb in its base form to describe regular past habits or states that do not happen or are not true anymore.

b. In interrogative sentences, we use the structure _____ + subject + _____ + the main verb in its base form. In short answers, either *did* or *didn't* is used.

c. In _____ sentences, we use the structure _____ *use to* + the main verb in its base form.

4. Answer the questions with *used to* or *didn't use to*.

a. Do you think air travel used to be more pleasant in the past? Why (not)?
_____
_____

b. In your opinion, how did travelers use to plan their trips in the past? How do they plan their trips nowadays?
_____
_____

c. What did you use to do before and while traveling in the past that you don't do anymore?
_____
_____

EXPAND YOUR READING

1. Read part of an article on packing and complete the infographic.

How To Travel Anywhere With Nothing But A Carry-On Bag
Deborah L. Jacobs — Forbes Staff

Whether you are packing for a business trip or going on vacation, it pays to travel light.
The trade-off is that you must live with less, which involves what may seem like some tough choices about what stays and what goes. No matter how long you are away for, pack just one week's worth of clothing. Here's how to think–and pack–like a minimalist.

1. Put things in perspective.

To pack light, you must be willing to live with less. If that makes you uncomfortable, remember it's only temporary; consider it a vacation from your possessions.

2. Choose a capacious carry-on.

Whatever bag you choose sets the limit on how much you can take: if it doesn't fit, it doesn't go. On the other hand, don't feel you must fill every available crevice. You will welcome the extra space for those must-have souvenirs.

3. Bring ample footwear.

Figure out what's appropriate for the activities you have planned. When I need to bring hiking boots or winter boots, I wear them on trains and planes, and carry a pair of ballet slippers in my purse to change into once I'm on board. The only footwear that goes in my suitcase is a pair of sneakers or comfortable walking shoes, and a set of flip flops that I use as bedroom slippers, to pad around hotels, and when going to the beach or swimming pool.

4. Be a minimalist with toiletries.

Pare your list down to what you absolutely need.

5. Layer to change your look.

This approach gives you more outfits and the flexibility to adjust for weather changes–for example if your trip takes you to various climate zones, or you run into a heat wave or cold snap. For example, one long-sleeve button-down shirt, two camisoles, two tank tops and a cardigan can be combined in multiple ways.

Adapted from www.forbes.com/sites/deborahljacobs/2013/07/29/how-to-travel-anywhere-with-nothing-but-a-carry-on-bag/. Accessed on August 8, 2018.

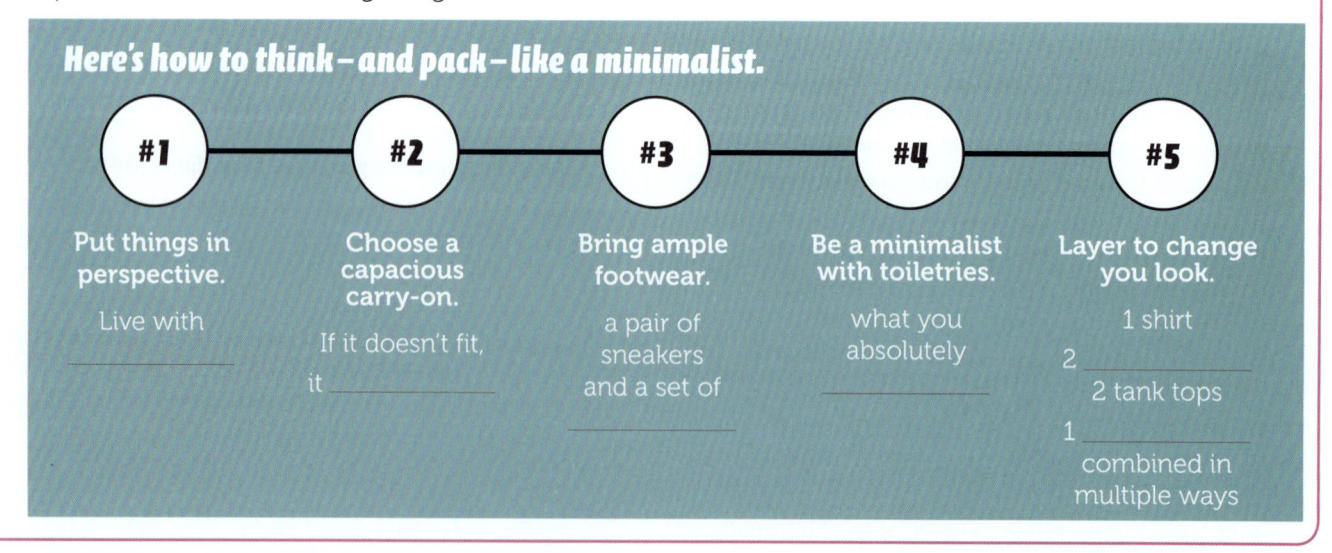

Here's how to think – and pack – like a minimalist.

#1	#2	#3	#4	#5
Put things in perspective.	Choose a capacious carry-on.	Bring ample footwear.	Be a minimalist with toiletries.	Layer to change you look.
Live with _____	If it doesn't fit, it _____	a pair of sneakers and a set of _____	what you absolutely _____	1 shirt / 2 _____ / 2 tank tops / 1 _____ combined in multiple ways

2. Underline the option that best completes the description. Infographics...

   a. are sets of drawings containing commentaries expressing the author's opinion about a topic often associated with politics or social issues.

   b. are visual representations of information in the forms of images and texts intended to provide readers with an easier comprehension of often complex subjects.

LANGUAGE IN USE 2

Unit 8

MODAL VERB – MUST

1. Check (✓) the sentence that has a similar meaning to this extract from the infographic on page 76.

   > [...] you **must** live with less.

   ( ) It's possible to live with less.
   ( ) It's necessary to live with less.
   ( ) It's correct to live with less.

2. Match the modal verbs in bold in the sentences below to the ideas they convey.

   a. Drivers and car passengers **must** wear a seatbelt.
   b. So you're a travel agent? That **must** be very interesting!
   c. One **must not** use a handheld cell phone while driving.

   ( ) prohibition
   ( ) obligation
   ( ) deduction

3. Read the text and use *must* or *mustn't* and the verbs from the box to fill in the blanks.

   > be   bring   obey   travel

   ### TRAVEL TIPS

   Things you _____ with if you are leaving on a flight

   Africa is an amazing place to be and exotic for those who want to spend their vacation here. However, it can be a nightmare for foreigners who end up on the wrong side of the law. Before you make your way to Africa, make sure that you have understood the local laws and abide by these rules and regulations.

   African airports may not be as digitally advanced as airports in more developed countries. You may think that these airports are not strict or governed by rules you _____. However, you are expected to be on your best behavior and never find yourself in the line of fire of lawyers or the local police by running the risk of getting yourself arrested. These are some of the things you _____ to the airport.

   Excessive Money

   You may be a business person, but it is expected that you handle your business transactions online. Money laundering is a serious crime. There is a limit on the amount of money you are expected to carry with you.

   Countries have different rules about receiving money in their airports.

   [...]

   Live Animals

   No matter how much you love your kids, they will always grow and become independent. However, if you love your pets and you want to travel with them, you _____ sure the airport you are going to use does not have a restriction.

   Fresh Food

   You are not allowed to travel in or out with fresh products like fruits, vegetables, and eggs.

   Precious Metals

   Customs officers demand that you present to them for assessment any precious metals that you have bought. They would be the ones to talk to concerning the rules about those precious metals that may be imported and those that may be taken out.

   [...]

   Adapted from www.momoafrica.com/things-you-mustnt-travel-with-if-you-are-leaving-with-a-flight. Accessed on June 10, 2018.

4. Based on the discussions throughout this unit, write a new tip for packing wisely.

   In order to pack wisely, you must _____
   _____

LISTENING COMPREHENSION

1. **Look at the book covers below. What do all these books have in common?**
   _____

   Ghost Train to the Eastern Star | **Travels with Charley** | **The Road to Oxiana**

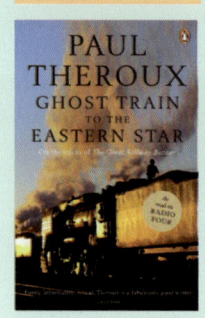

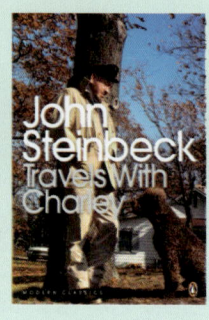

2. **You are going to listen to part of the radio program *Talk of the Nation*, in which the American journalist Neal Conan talks to and about Paul Theroux. Listen to the first part and complete the transcript with the missing information.**

   This is Talk of the Nation. I'm Neal Conan in Washington. In 1973, Paul Theroux said goodbye to his wife and children in London and set off on a _____ that would make his career and change his life. Theroux was a novelist then, out of ideas, and he hoped that a trip across Europe and Asia and back would inspire a new book. Theroux boarded the Golden Arrow, took the ferry to France, transferred to the _____, and rode the _____ east to Iran and Afghanistan, India, Burma, Vietnam, China, and Japan, then home again through the length of the Soviet Union. It took him four and a half months, and he then wrote a now classic book, "The Great Railway Bazaar," which many credit as the start of a new kind of travel _____.

   More than three decades later, Theroux retraced his steps as much as he could. There are new train routes, different landscapes, new borders, and different political realities, and he chronicles that trip in his new book, "Ghost _____ to the Eastern Star." If you'd like to talk with Paul Theroux about his _____, about what's changed, and what hasn't, along the way, our phone number is 800-989-8255. The email address is talk@npr.org, and you can join the conversation on our blog. That's at npr.org/blogofthenation. While you're there, you can go to our blog and read an excerpt from "Ghost Train to the Eastern Star." That's at npr.org/blogofthenation.

   [...]

   Extracted from www.npr.org/templates/story/story.php?storyId=93702596.
   Accessed on June 10, 2018.

3. **Listen to another part of the program, read the sentences below, and circle the correct alternatives to complete them.**

   a. At the beginning of Theroux's *Ghost Train to the Eastern Star*, he describes traveling as one of the **cheapest / easiest** ways of passing time.

   b. Conan tells Theroux that many of their listeners will remember him as a marvelous **travel agent / traveling companion** 35 years ago.

   c. In Theroux's opinion, travelers **must / must not** be optimistic and in a fairly good mood.

4. **Listen to the last part of the talk, in which Mr. Theroux explains why he thinks luxury is the enemy of observation in travels. Then work with a partner to answer the questions: Do you agree that someone can travel around quite cheaply if he / she gives up opulence? In your opinion, what really matters when it comes to traveling? Report your opinions to the class.**

≫ EXPAND YOUR HORIZONS ≫≫≫

Check (✓) the column that best describes your opinion about each statement. Then discuss your answers with your classmates and teacher, justifying your point of view.

	I agree.	I'm not sure.	I disagree.
a. Packing wisely equals traveling happily, saving more time, money, and annoyance.			
b. Air travels in economy cabins will only get worse because airlines will keep opting to cram more and more travelers into a plane.			
c. One will never be the same again after going on a journey, be it a luxurious or a modest one.			

REVIEW 4

Unit 7 and 8

1. **Read the dictionary entry and the title of the text below. What do you think the text is about? Exchange ideas with a classmate.** *Predicting the theme*

   peak
   1 [usually singular] the time when something or someone is best, greatest, highest, most successful, etc.

   Adapted from www.ldoceonline.com/dictionary/peak. Accessed on July 18, 2018.

   ---

   www.theguardian.com/commentisfree/2018/feb/27/reached-peak-english-britain-china

   News | Opinion | Sport | Culture | Lifestyle

   ## Have we reached peak English in the world?
   Nicholas Ostler

   In China last month, Theresa May attended the **launch** of the British Council's English is Great campaign, intended to **boost** interest and fluency in our national language. This might sound like Donald Trump's notorious "Make America great again", but comes in fact from a stronger position. **Beyond doubt**, the use of English is greater than ever, and far more **widespread** than any other language in the world. All non-English-speaking powers of our globalized world
   5 recognize it as the first foreign language to learn; it is also, uniquely, in practical use worldwide. The British Council **reckons** that English is spoken at a useful level by some 1.75 billion people, a quarter of the world's population. It is taught from primary level up in all China's schools; it is the working language of the whole European Union.

   […]

   This global acceptance of English, now far beyond the zones of influence of the British Empire or the United States' backyard, has effectively grown up in just a century – **neatly**, and a little paradoxically, since the 1919 treaty of
   10 Versailles. In deference to that of the U.S., this was the first international treaty written in English; but it also turned out to mark the incipient decline of the world's greatest English-speaking institution, the British Empire. From a language point of view, however, British power had the good fortune to be succeeded by its cousin in North America, so that the usual historic **lag**, as political command leads on to linguistic imitation, was disguised. Even as Britain began to decline economically, its established position was reflected by increased take-up of English as the language to learn.

   15 But all this while, especially from the 1920s to the 1990s, the focus of U.S. expansion was changing, moving from North America to the world, leading to influence on trade, engineering, telecommunications, mining, media, science, and finance, as the dollar moved to replace sterling as the world's reserve currency. This was followed by the digital information revolution, creating new fortunes based in Silicon Valley at the turn of the 21st century. These were all positive for the world role of English (a role founded by Great Britain), but should have been
   20 expected to peak later, in the growth of soft power and the increased popularity of American culture.

   It is this lagged growth of English, reflecting U.S. influence **hitherto**, that we are now experiencing. Yet it is happening in a 21st century when other nations, particularly in Asia but also in South America and Africa, are far **outpacing** the USA (let alone Britain and the European Union) in economic growth rates. This is an amazing juncture in world history. And two questions arise. Is the position of English a real asset to the states that speak it natively? And is the language likely to hold this position in the **pecking order** indefinitely?

   […]

   Adapted from www.theguardian.com/commentisfree/2018/feb/27/reached-peak-english-britain-china. Accessed on June 29, 2018.

2. **Check (✓) the statements that are <u>not</u> true according to the text.** *Understanding details*
   a. ( ) When circumstances change, dominant languages fall.
   b. ( ) Some nations still resist and choose not to accept English as the language to be learned.
   c. ( ) The influence of English has risen immensely in just 100 years.
   d. ( ) Britain's current economic power is the cause of success of English as the global language.
   e. ( ) The economies of countries in South America, Africa, and Asia are growing more than that of the U.S.

3. **Read the sentences below, extracted from the text on the previous page, and circle the possessive 's (or genitive case).**
   a. "[...] Theresa May attended the launch of the British Council's English is Great campaign, [...]"
   b. "[...] This might sound like Donald Trump's notorious "Make America great again", [...]"
   c. "[...] It is taught from primary level up in all China's schools; it is the working language of the whole European Union. [...]"
   d. "[...] This global acceptance of English, now far beyond the zones of influence of the British Empire or the United States' backyard. [...]"

4. **Complete the following sentences with the correct possessive pronouns.**
   a. I need to fix my suitcase and you need to fix _____, too.
   b. She has already arrived at her final destination. He has arrived at _____, too.
   c. Our zipper tab is broken. Ann and Jeff told me _____ is broken, too.
   d. No, this is their baggage. Is this _____, honey?

5. **Read the comic strips. Then complete them with the correct form of *used to* followed by the main verbs *come* or *be*.**

6. **Rewrite the following sentences with *must*.**
   a. You have to have duct tape when you travel in case you need to fix your suitcase.

   _____

   _____

   b. It is very likely that one of the passengers will have duct tape.

   _____

GRAMMAR OVERVIEW

Verb tenses

Tense	Use(s)	Example(s) affirmative	Example(s) negative	Example(s) interrogative
Simple present	• Habits; • Routines; • Timeless events; • Narratives; • Scheduled events; • With frequency adverbs (e.g. *always*, *never*); • With stative verbs.	I **go** to school in the morning. Our class always **starts** at 8. I **am** very happy today.	I **do not / don't go** to school in the afternoon. Our class **does not / doesn't** usually **start** at 7. She **is not / isn't** very happy today.	When **do** you **go** to school? **Does** your class always **start** at 8? **Is** he always happy?
Present continuous	• Actions in progress in the present; • With action verbs.	They **are playing** basketball now. Daisy **is making** lunch.	They **are not / aren't playing** video games now. Daisy **is not / isn't making** a lot of food for lunch.	**Are** they **playing** sports now? **Is** Daisy **making** lunch for us?
Imperative form	• Ask for favors (informal); • Give commands.	**Open** the window (please).	**Do not / Don't close** the window (please). It's hot.	**Close** the window, will you?
Simple past	• Completed actions in the past; • Sequence of events in the past; • With past time expressions (e.g., *yesterday*, *last month*).	I **studied** in the morning. Then I **went** to the park. He **had** lunch at home yesterday.	Doug **did not / didn't study** with us. He **did not / didn't have** pizza for lunch.	**Did** you **study** for your test? Where **did** they **have** lunch?

Pronouns

Pronouns	Form	Use	Example(s)
Subject pronouns	I / you / he / she / it / we / they	Before the main verb to replace the subject	**I** am thankful for your help. **She** didn't work much last week.
Object pronouns	me / you / him / her / it / us / them	After the main verb to replace the object	I can't help **him**. I'm sorry. Can I go to the party with **them**?
Possessive adjectives	my / your / his / her / its / our / their	Before nouns to refer to possession	This is **my** car. Do you want a ride? When is **your** birthday?
Possessive pronouns	mine / yours / his / hers / its / ours / theirs	Before verbs; At the end of a clause.	This is my jacket. **Hers** is red, not blue. Your house is much bigger than **mine**.

GRAMMAR OVERVIEW

Modal verbs

Modal verb	Use(s)	Example(s) affirmative	Example(s) negative	Example(s) interrogative
Can	• Ability; • Permission; • Possibility; • Requests; • Offers; • Prohibition (*can't*).	I **can run** very fast. Of course she **can come** to visit us!	I **cannot / can't swim** well. You **cannot / can't drive** without a license.	**Can** he **run** fast, too? **Can** I **use** the restroom? **Can** I **help** you?
Could	• Ability in the past; • Formal requests; • Suggestions; • Possibility.	We **could go** to the movies.	She **could not / couldn't dance** before, but now she is a pro!	**Could** you **tell** me the way to the airport?
Should	• Advice; • Suggestions; • Ideal situations.	You **should take** an aspirin for your headache. People **should be** respectful toward nature.	You **should not / shouldn't eat** too much. He **should not / shouldn't spend** so much money on clothes.	**Should** I **call** her? What **should** we all **do** to take care of nature?
Must	• Obligation; • Prohibition; • Deduction (affirmative only); • Laws and rules.	We **must carry** an ID at all times. You **must be** very tired after all that exercise!	You **must not drink** and **drive**!	**Do** I have to **go**? I don't want to.
Used to	• A state in the past; • Habit or regular activity in the past.	They **used to see** each other every day. Now they never meet up	We **didn't use to be** friends, but now we get along.	**Did** John **use to** be a good student? How many hours **did** you **use to spend** in front of the TV?

Plural of nouns

Case	Plural form	Example(s)
Plural with *s*	Add *s* to the noun.	house**s**, cat**s**, newspaper**s**
Plural with *es*	Add *es* to nouns ending in *s* / *sh* / *ch* / *x*.	bus**es**, dish**es**, match**es**, box**es**
Plural with *ies*	Remove *y* and add *ies* to nouns ending in consonant + *y*.	bab**ies**, cit**ies**
Irregular plurals	Use a different word to refer to plural; Some words finishing in *s* have the same word for plural.	child – children person – people man – men news – news gymnastics – gymnastics
Collective nouns	Use to refer to a group of a given noun.	musicians – band people – crowd students – class

's for possession (genitive case)

Case	Form and use	Example(s)
's	Add 's to singular nouns to refer to possession; Add 's to irregular plurals to refer to possession;	This is Lisa's book. The children's room is a mess!
'	Add only ' to regular plurals; Add only ' to names ending in s.	The students' grades are bad. They all need to review the content. I love James' new house! It's small and cozy.
of	Use the preposition *of* when the possession refers to inanimate beings (not people or animals).	The roof **of** the house is brown. The battery **of** the telephones last for a very short time nowadays.

Prefixes

Prefix	Meaning	Example(s)
auto-	self	**auto**biography
inter-	between	**inter**planetary
mid-	middle	**mid**day
out-	go beyond	**out**perform
over-	too much	**over**weight
post-	after	**post**-graduation
pre-	before	**pre**view
under-	less	**under**achieve

Suffixes

Suffix	Forms a(n)	Example(s)
-able	adjective	avail**able**
-ive	adjective	informat**ive**
-al	adjective / noun	classic**al** / surviv**al**
-ful	adjective	help**ful**
-ish	adjective	child**ish**
-less	adjective	use**less**
-ous	adjective	gener**ous**
-y	adjective	snow**y**
-ance	noun	appear**ance**
-ation / -tion	noun	applic**ation**
-sion	noun	illu**sion**
-ure	noun	proced**ure**
-ment	noun	argu**ment**
-age	noun	herit**age**

GRAMMAR OVERVIEW

Comparative and superlative forms

Structure	Form	Example(s)
Comparative of superiority: one or two-syllable adjectives	Add –er to the adjective (+ than)	My sister is tall**er than** me. Math equations were **easier** in the past (**than** they are now).
Comparative of superiority: nouns, adverbs ending in –ly, and three- or four-syllable adjectives	Add *more* before the adjective / noun (+ *than*)	I eat **more** vegetables now **than** when I was a child. He walks **more** slowly **than** his mom. That leaflet is **more** informative **than** the one they had last year.
Comparative of superiority: irregular adjectives	good – better bad – worse far – farther / further little – less	I find this movie way **better than** the one we watched last night. We can go to that store, but it's **farther than** the one we usually go to.
Double comparatives	The (comparative)… the (comparative)	**The more** I try, **the easier** it gets. **The more, the better!**
Superlative of superiority: one or two-syllable adjectives	Add *the* or possessive adjective before the adjective and –*est* to the adjective	It is **the** larg**est** pizza I have ever eaten! That was **my** fast**est** trip! It took only five minutes.
Superlative of superiority: three- or four-syllable adjectives	Add *the most* before the adjective	Wow! This is **the most** comfortable armchair I have sat on! They have **the most** delicious food in the city.

Word categories

Category	Form / Examples in words	Meaning	Examples in a sentence
Slang and informal terms about relationships	1. Dump 2. Have a crush on	1. To end a relationship with someone. 2. Someone you have romantic feelings for, but not are not in a relationship with.	Did you hear the last news? George **dumped** Amy! OK, I'll tell you the truth. **I have a crush on** your brother.
Idioms	1. It's all Greek to me. 2. Loaded language	1. Used to say that you cannot understand something. 2. Persuasive language	What's this new software? **It's all Greek to me!** Don't come to me with this **loaded language**. I know your true intentions.
Phrasal verbs	Verb + one or two prepositions / adverbs	The meaning of phrasal verbs can sometimes be literal, but it can also be very different from the meaning of the two or three words read separately.	I need to go the gym and **work out**. The hotel manager said that we can **check in** an hour earlier.

Adjectives – word order

Opinion	Size	Physical quality	Age	Shape	Color	Origin	Material	Type	Purpose
beautiful	small	unmarked	old	square	blue	Italian	paper	bilingual	dictionary
It's a **lovely old wooden** house.									
I have two **square blue vintage** tables.									

LANGUAGE REFERENCE

UNIT 1

SIMPLE PRESENT

Usage Notes

The simple present is often used to refer to:

- present facts or timeless events;

    Why **does** migration **occur**?

    Migration **occurs** because of economic, political, social, religious, and other different reasons.

- habits, routines, and repeated actions in the present.

    In some schools, English classes **don't take place** in regular classrooms. Students **attend** classes in language labs.

Forms

- Affirmative sentences use the verb in its base form unless the subject is the third person singular (*he*, *she*, *it*); in this case, *-s* or *-es* is added.

    A healthy life **includes** more than having a balanced diet and exercising. It **means** balance!

- Verbs in the third person singular (*he*, *she*, *it*) follow these spelling rules:

    – if the verb ends in *-ss*, *-x*, *-ch*, *-sh*, *-o* add *-es*;

    kiss – kisses
    fix – fixes
    watch – watches

    – if the verb ends with a *consonant + y*, remove the *-y* and add *-ies*.

    study – studies
    hurry – hurries

- Negative sentences use an auxiliary verb followed by the main verb in its base form. When the subject is *I*, *you*, *we*, or *they*, *do not* (*don't*) is used.
    When the subject is **he, she, or it**, *does not* (*doesn't*) is used.

    Globalization **doesn't increase** borders between nations. On the contrary, nations **don't seem** so distant these days, thanks to the Internet.

- Note that when the subject is *he, she, it,* the main verb is used in its base form:

    Globalization **doesn't increase** borders between nations.

    NOT   Globalization ~~doesn't increases~~ borders between nations.

IMPERATIVE

Usage Notes

- When we make requests it's more polite to use a modal verb instead of the imperative.

    "Could you open the window?" is more polite than "**Open** the window, please."

- To make imperatives sound less direct we can use *please*, for example.

    "**Stop** talking, please." is less direct than "**Stop** talking."

- To add emphasis and be more direct, we may use subjects in imperatives.

    Everybody **look** at the board!

    Don't you **pretend** not to know me! We were classmates last year.

ADJECTIVE SUFFIXES

Suffixes are letters added to the end of a word to form new words. Below is a list of suffixes that change verbs and nouns into adjectives.

Verb + Suffix	Examples
rely + -able	reliable
create + -ive	creative
Noun + Suffix	**Examples**
misery + -able	miserable
music + -al	musical
pain + -ful	painful
hero + -ic	heroic
self + -ish	selfish
effect + -ive	effective
end + -less	endless
fame + -ous	famous
wind + -y	windy

Usage Notes

- Adjectives ending in *-ical* and *-ic* often have different meanings, for example:

LANGUAGE REFERENCE

- *classic* means typical, admired, very good, while *classical* means traditional;
- *economic* means relating to trade, industry, and the management of money, while *economical* means using money, time, goods, etc., carefully and without wasting any;
- *historic* can mean very important, while *historical* means related to the past.

▶ UNIT 2

SIMPLE PRESENT

Usage Notes

Besides the common usages listed on page 85, the simple present may also be used:

- in narratives or descriptions of past events.

    Next thing I **know**, I **slip** on a banana peel and **fall** to the ground. Then I **look** around, **pretend** nothing **bothers** me, **get** up, and **head** to the restroom.

- to talk about scheduled events.

    The field trip bus **leaves** at 7 A.M. next Tuesday.

Form

- Interrogative sentences use an auxiliary verb before the subject and the main verb in its base form. When the subject is *I, you, we,* or *they, do* is used. When the subject is *he, she,* or *it, does* is used.

    Do you **have** any questions?
    Does the teacher **need** our help with the classroom organization?

- However, in information questions, when the subject is the answer to the question, the main verb in the simple present form is used.

    Who **lives** with you?
    What **makes** your life happier?

- Note that when the subject is *he, she, it,* the main verb is used in its base form.

    Does the teacher **need** our help with the classroom organization?

    NOT ~~Does the teacher needs our help with the classroom organization?~~

FREQUENCY ADVERBS

Usage Notes

Frequency adverbs describe when or how often something is done. There are two types of frequency adverbs: definite frequency and indefinite frequency adverbs.

- Adverbs of definite frequency such as *last month*, *every day*, and *once a week*, often take the end position; they are <u>not</u> placed after the verb *be* and before regular verbs as indefinite frequency adverbs such as *always*, *never*, and *usually*.

    I have English classes **twice a week**.
    I **sometimes** visit my relatives in the country.
    Britney's parents pick her up at school **every day**.
    Cooks **often** refer to themselves as chefs.
    Lennon was the best student in class **last year**.
    I am **never** late for class.

IDIOMS ABOUT HEALTH

Idioms are a group of words that has a special meaning that is different from the ordinary meaning of each separate word.

Idiom	Meaning	Example
a bag of bones	someone who is much too thin	He's lost too much weight because of his illness. He's **a bag of bones** these days.
a clean bill of health	a report that says you are healthy or that a machine or building is safe	Inspectors gave our school **a clean bill of health**.
kick the bucket	to die – used humorously	Uncle Jerry was so appalled by what he saw that he almost **kicked the bucket**.
safe and sound	unharmed, especially after being in danger	The missing teens are back home **safe and sound**.
under the knife	having a medical operation	Men and women go **under the knife** to enhance their looks.

Based on from www.ldoceonline.com/dictionary. Accessed on August 20, 2018.

PHRASAL VERBS ABOUT HEALTH

Phrasal verbs are "a group of words that is used like a verb and consists of a verb with an adverb or preposition after it […]"

Phrasal Verb	Meaning	Example
come down with	to get an illness	I've been sneezing all morning. I think I'm **coming down with** the flu.

Phrasal Verb	Meaning	Example
get over	to become well again after an illness	Dad can't seem to **get over** his cold.
pass away	to die	Sadly, Peter's uncle **passed away**.
throw up	to bring food or drink up from your stomach out through your mouth because you are ill	Just the thought of coffee makes me feel like **throwing up**.
work out	to make your body fit and strong by doing exercises	Bodybuilders **work out** for several hours a day.

Based on www.ldoceonline.com/dictionary. Accessed on August 20, 2018.

UNIT 3
PRESENT CONTINUOUS AND SIMPLE PRESENT: STATIVE VS. ACTION VERBS

Usage Notes

A few verbs are rarely used in the present continuous form because they describe states or situations that are not expected to change. They are called stative verbs as they do not describe actions. Stative verbs may indicate:

- feelings and emotions (*dislike, like, love, need, appreciate, want, hate, wish,* etc.);

  I **dislike** math but I **love** English.

- senses (*smell, hear, see, taste, seem,* etc.);

  I'm afraid that cake **doesn't smell** good.

- possessions (*have, belong, possess, own,* etc.);

  This house **belongs** to my grandma.

- opinions, knowledge, or beliefs (*mean, believe, doubt, imagine, think, guess, know, understand,* etc.).

  I **don't believe** that the manager is right this time.

Other common stative verbs are:

- be

  They're physicians.

- concern

  That issue **concerns** all 9th grade students.

- consist

  The test **consists** of 5 open-ended questions.

- cost

  Those fancy shirts **cost** a fortune!

- depend

  Our decision about the trip **depends** on the weather.

- fit

  Your plans **don't fit** the family schedule.

- involve

  Being healthy **involves** real hard work.

- lack

  The teacher said my writing **lacks** cohesion.

- matter

  Does it really **matter** what he thinks about you?

Some verbs describe both a state and an action and are used in the simple present or in the present continuous, respectively.

- feel

  I **don't feel** I should try to call him again.

  I'm **feeling** terrible right now

- see

  I **see** your point.

  They're **seeing** a marriage counselor.

- think

  He **thinks** they are better than us.

  He's **thinking** about moving abroad.

- appear

  Your prediction **appears** to be true.

  That famous actress **is appearing** in a new commercial.

- look

  This **looks** amazing!

  We're **looking** at the stars and making wishes.

- taste

  Her food **tastes** delicious!

  The chefs **are tasting** the contestants' dishes.

FALSE FRIENDS

Examples	Meaning
agenda	a list of the subjects to be discussed at a meeting
attend	to go to an event such as a meeting or a class
college	a large school where you can study after high school and get a degree

LANGUAGE REFERENCE

Examples	Meaning
costume	a set of clothes worn by an actor or by someone to make them look like something or someone else, such as an animal, famous person, etc.
curse	swear
eventually	after a long time, or after a lot of things have happened
intend	to have something in your mind as a plan or purpose
legend	an old well-known story, often about brave people, adventures, or magical events
particular	certain, specific
prescribe	to say what medicine or treatment a sick person should have
retired	having stopped working, usually because of your age
turn	to move your body so that you are looking in a different direction

Based on www.ldoceonline.com/dictionary. Accessed on August 20, 2018.

▶ UNIT 4

SIMPLE PAST

Usage Notes

The simple past is used to refer to:

- completed actions in the past;
  Where **did** the family reunion **take place**?
  We **met** at Britany's.
  They **didn't remember** to call us.

- a series of completed actions in the past;
  I **woke up** at 6, **took** a shower, **had** breakfast, and then **left** for work.

- an action that started and finished in the past;
  We **spoke** for half an hour.
  They **didn't live** in Rome for very long.

Pronunciation of -ed endings

For regular verbs, -ed endings are pronounced:

- /d/ after all vowel sounds and after voiced consonants (except /d/)
  /m/ /n/ /ŋ/ /l/ /g/ /dʒ/ /z/ /b/ /v/;
  enjoyed, tried, smiled, lived

- /t/ after all voiceless consonants (except /t/)
  /k/ /p/ /f/ /s/ /ʃ/ /tʃ/;
  shopped, laughed, crossed, wished

- /ɪd/ after /d/ and /t/.
  needed, decided, hated, started

MODAL VERBS

Modal verbs are auxiliary verbs used to add to or change meanings of main verbs. *Can, should, must, may,* and *could* are examples of modal verbs. Modal verbs are different from regular verbs because:

- they are followed by an infinitive without "to" (except for *ought to*);
- they don't take -s in the third person singular;
- they are used like auxiliaries for questions and negatives.

MODAL VERB - CAN

Usage Notes

We use *can* or *cannot* (*can't*) for:

- permission;
  Can I talk to you for a second?

- prohibition;
  Students **can't** use dictionaries during tests.

- ability;
  Harry **can** speak four languages fluently.

- general truths;
  Leading a healthy life **can** be difficult, but the hard work will pay off in the future.

- possibility;
  Larry **can** help you with the interview because he has worked in PR.

- guessing and predicting;
  This awful test **can't** be mine! I'm sure I did a good job.

- requests;
  Can I see your passport, please?

- offers;
  Can I help you carry those bags?

- reproaches.
  Can't you stop making that noise? I'm trying to concentrate here!

We also use *can* with verbs of perception such as *see, hear, taste, smell,* and other verbs such as *imagine, guess,* and *follow* when they mean *understand*.

I **can** guess why you look so upset.
I **can** hear you.

MODAL VERB - *SHOULD*

Usage Notes

Some common uses of *should* are:

- for advice or suggestions;

    You **should** cut down on sugar if you have diabetes.

- to talk about what is ideal or desirable;

    There **should** be a dedicated entrance for the elderly in this stadium.

- to talk about what is likely to happen;

    Let's start our discussions. The other students **should** be here soon.

- for possibilities in hypothetical conditional sentences;

    Should you want to contact me, there's a private number you can call.

- to express gratitude.

    A: Lisa, I bought you a handmade scarf.

    B: Oh, you **shouldn't** have!

SLANG OR INFORMAL TERMS ABOUT RELATIONSHIPS

Examples	Meaning
catfish	someone who lies about themselves on the Internet in order to impress people, especially so that someone will start a relationship with them
dump	to end a relationship with someone
frenemy	someone you have a friendly relationship with, but who is really an enemy or competitor
have a crush on	someone you have a feeling of romantic love for, but who you do not know well
hit on somebody	to talk to someone in a way that shows you are sexually attracted to them
pop the question	to ask someone to marry you
top dog	the person who has the most power in a group, especially after a struggle

Based on www.ldoceonline.com/dictionary. Accessed on August 20, 2018.

UNIT 5

PLURAL NOUNS

Usage Notes

- Some nouns keep the same forms for singular or plural forms. Seeing them in context is the key to identifying them as singular or plural.

    fish, sheep, series, species, deer, etc.

- Some nouns only have a plural form.

    clothes, contents, dislikes, glasses, pants, jeans, pajamas, scissors, shorts, stairs, likes, etc.

- Some nouns are used only in the singular form, although they end in *-s*.

    classics, economics, physics, gymnastics, aerobics, measles, news, etc.

- Collective nouns name groups of people and may take a singular verb if they are considered a single unit or a plural verb if they are considered a collection of individuals. Some common collective nouns are:

    army, audience, committee, company, crew, family, government, jury, etc.

- Other collective nouns are:

band	musicians
board	directors
choir	singers
class	students
crowd	people
gang	thieves
team	players
bouquet	flowers
fleet	ships
forest	trees
galaxy	stars
pack	cards
range	mountains
army	ants
flock	birds
flock	sheep
hive	bees
pack	wolves

LANGUAGE REFERENCE

ADJECTIVES – WORD ORDER

Usage Notes

- When there is more than one adjective after a linking verb such as *be*, the last two adjectives are usually connected by *and*. However, *and* is less common when those adjectives come before the noun they qualify.

    Linda is **happy**, **young**, **and Greek**. You'll like her, for sure.

    Linda has always been **a happy**, **young**, **Greek** girl.

- The connector *and* can be used when there are two or more adjectives of the same type as well.

    That was a **lovely and unusual** dinner.

    Have you seen my **yellow and green** sneakers?

PREFIXES

Some other common prefixes in English.

Prefix	Meaning	Example
auto-	self	autoimmunity
inter-	between	international
mega-	very big, important	megapixel
mid-	middle	midnight
out-	go beyond	outbreak
over-	too much	overdose
post-	after	post-war
pre-	before	prehistoric
trans-	across	transformation
under-	less than, beneath	underestimate
up-	make or move higher	upstairs

UNIT 6

COMPARATIVES AND SUPERLATIVES

Usage Note

- Some adjectives do not have a comparative or superlative form because they can't show a greater or lesser amount.
  These are called absolute adjectives. A few examples are: adequate, complete, dead, fatal, ideal, impossible, infinite, perfect, universal, round, and unique.

    She is a unique woman and I admire her a lot.

  NOT   She is the most unique woman I have ever met.

    These games are perfect for learning.

  NOT   They are the most perfect games for learning.

DOUBLE COMPARATIVES

- Double comparatives are used to express increasing or decreasing degrees.

    The more I work, **the more** I want to work.

    The less time I spend here, **the more** spare time I'll have.

    The harder the task, **the fiercer** I become.

    The more you explain, **the more** they learn.

    The older you get, **the more experienced** you get.

Usage Note

In spoken English, some double comparatives are usually shortened.

   The more the merrier.

   The sooner the better.

IRREGULAR COMPARATIVES AND SUPERLATIVES

Regular form	Comparative form	Superlative form
bad	worse	the worst
far (distance)	farther	the farthest
far (extent)	further	the furthest
good	better	the best
less	lesser	the least
little	less	the least
many / much	more	the most

VERB TO NOUN SUFFIXES

Verb + suffix	Examples
arrive + -al	arrival
accept + -ance	acceptance
declare + -ation / -tion	declaration
confuse + -sion	confusion
fail + -ure	failure
punish + -ment	punishment
marry + -age	marriage
bless + -ing	blessing
bake + -ery	bakery

UNIT 7

'S FOR POSSESSION

Usage Notes

's and ' can also be used in the following situations:

- when it is not necessary to repeat a noun;
  She is not my sister. She is Anna's.
- when we are referring to somebody's home or store;
  We're spending the holidays at our grandma's.
- with places;
  Rio's levels of violence are increasing.
- with time expressions.
  Yesterday's episode was amazing.
  I'm sure we'll meet in two weeks' time!
- When the owner is a thing and not a person or an animal, we often use the structure noun + of + noun.
  The leg of the table is broken.
- In this case, it is also possible to use the structure noun + noun.
  The table leg is broken.
- When the owner is longer or when it's a descriptive fragment, we don't use 's. We use of.
  The father of the student who failed the finals is waiting in the hall.

POSSESSIVE PRONOUNS

Usage Note

- Possessive pronouns are also used in the construction a friend / neighbor / student / of mine, of yours, etc. In this structure, the friend, neighbor, or student is a little more general, distant, or non-specific than when possessive adjectives are used (my friend, my neighbor, my student).

(Non-specific)

A cousin of mine is coming to visit us on the weekend.

(Specific)

My cousin is coming to visit us on the weekend.

IDIOMS ABOUT LANGUAGE

Idiom	Meaning
beyond words	astonishing situation where a person can't find the right words to express his/her emotions
in plain English/language	in clear and simple words, without using technical language
it goes without saying	a thing that is so obvious that it is not necessary to mention
it's all Greek to me	used to say that you cannot understand something
loaded language	persuasive language
speak the same language	if two people or groups speak the same language, they have similar attitudes and opinions
talk a mile a minute	talk very fast
talk is cheap	used to say that you do not believe someone will do what they say

Based on www.ldoceonline.com/dictionary. Accessed on August 20, 2018.

LANGUAGE REFERENCE

UNIT 8
USED TO

Usage Notes

- We use *used to* + *infinitive* to talk about a habit, a regular activity, or state in the past.

  They **used to** live in the suburbs.
  (= They do not live in the suburbs anymore.)

- Besides *used to*, *would* can also be used to talk about repeated past actions. But *would* isn't used when we talk about past states.

  I **used to** ride my bike to school on weekdays.
  I **would** ride my bike to school on weekdays.
  I **used to** love field trips when I was in younger.
  NOT ~~I would love field trips when I was in younger.~~

MODAL VERB - *MUST*

Usage Notes

We use *must* for:

- deductions and conclusions;

  Harry is late. He **must** be stuck in traffic.

- obligation and necessity;

  Policemen **must** wear a badge.

- laws and rules.

  Voters **must** present their voter card and a valid photo identification at the voting station.

- For invitations and encouragement, *have to* is more common than *must*.

  You **have to** try this carrot cake. It's pretty tasty!

- *Must not* and *don't have to* have different meanings. *Must not* means something is forbidden and *don't have to* means something is not necessary.

  You **must not** speak Portuguese in this class.
  You **don't have to** speak English all the time.

PHRASAL VERBS ABOUT TRAVELING

Phrasal Verb	Meaning	Example
check in / check out	if you check in or are checked in at a hotel or airport, you report that you have arrived; if you check out, you leave a hotel after paying the bill	We need to **check in** at least two hours before the fight.
drop off	take someone or something to a place by car and leave them there	Dad **dropped** me **off** on his way to the office.
get away	take a vacation away from the place you normally live	I'm really looking forward to **getting away** this weekend.
pack up	put things into cases, bags, etc. ready for a trip somewhere	Is there anyone to help me **pack up** for the trip?
see off	go to an airport, train station, etc. to say goodbye to someone	Claire has just left for the airport to **see** her boyfriend **off**.
set out	start a journey, especially a long journey	I'm **setting out** on a round-the-world tour next year.
stop over	stop somewhere and stay a short time before continuing a long journey	We are **stopping over** in São Paulo on the way to Lima.
take off	if an aircraft takes off, it rises into the air from the ground	I always get a bit anxious when the plane **takes off**.

Based on www.ldoceonline.com/dictionary. Accessed on August 20, 2018.

READING STRATEGIES

Ao longo da coleção, estamos sinalizando algumas estratégias de leitura voltadas à melhora na compreensão de textos. O principal objetivo dessas estratégias é fazer com que você, aluno, torne-se um aprendiz mais eficaz e alcance resultados positivos nos exames e vestibulares a serem realizados ao final do Ensino Médio.

A seguir você encontrará uma breve explicação sobre as estratégias mais comumente abordadas antes e durante a leitura dos textos.

Activating previous knowledge – Esta estratégia consiste em acionar, quando preciso, o conhecimento que você tem guardado em sua mente. Quando falamos em conhecimento prévio na leitura, estamos nos referindo às informações que você precisa ter para ler um texto sem muita dificuldade para compreendê-lo.

Brainstorming – O termo foi criado a partir da junção das palavras *brain* (cérebro) e *storm* (tempestade), portanto, significa "tempestade cerebral" ou "tempestade de ideias". A estratégia propõe que você e seus colegas de sala explorem sua capacidade criativa, na medida em que trocam ideias a respeito do assunto que será abordado no texto.

Bridging – O termo vem da palavra *bridge*, que significa "ponte". A estratégia consiste, então, em "fazer uma ponte", isto é, em estabelecer uma relação entre o seu conhecimento prévio sobre o assunto que será explorado no texto e o texto propriamente.

Finding organizational patterns or understanding text structure – A estrutura de um texto diz respeito à forma como as informações estão nele organizadas. Artigos, por exemplo, contam com uma introdução, um desenvolvimento e uma conclusão; as informações nas biografias são, em geral, organizadas em sequência cronológica; as receitas, na maioria das vezes, são divididas em duas partes – ingredientes e modo de preparo. Assim, estar atento aos padrões de organização de um texto ajuda-o a identificar seu gênero e, consequentemente, sua função social.

Predicting – A palavra *predict* significa "prever". Ao lermos o título de um texto ou observarmos as imagens que o acompanham, por exemplo, podemos prever ou deduzir seu conteúdo. Quanto mais conhecimento geral você tiver, mais facilmente vai prever o assunto de um texto. Em algumas atividades, você é convidado especificamente a prever o tema e o gênero do texto (*predicting the theme and the genre*).

Recognizing or identifying – Reconhecer significa identificar algo que se conhece. Portanto, reconhecer ou identificar o tipo textual (*textual type*), a voz, ou seja, quem está falando no texto (*voice in a text*), a perspectiva do autor (*the author's perspective*), a fonte do texto (*the source of the text*), o público ao qual o texto se destina (*the target audience*), o propósito principal do texto (*the main purpose*), etc. ajuda-o a antecipar o que está por vir no texto a ser lido.

Skimming – Consiste em observar o texto rapidamente para detectar o assunto geral ou o seu propósito geral (*skimming to identify the main purpose*), por exemplo. Nesse momento, não há nenhuma preocupação em se atentar aos detalhes. É importante que você observe o *layout* do texto, seu título e sub-títulos, cognatos, primeiras e últimas linhas de cada parágrafo, bem como as imagens, gráficos e tabelas que o acompanham.

Scanning - é uma técnica de leitura que consiste em correr rapidamente os olhos pelo texto até localizar a informação específica desejada. O *scanning* é prática rotineira na vida das pessoas. Alguns exemplos típicos pode. Alguns exemplos típicos são o uso do dicionário para obter informação sobre o significado de palavras ou a utilização do índice de um livro para encontrar um artigo ou capítulo de interesse.

Há, também, estratégias que são trabalhadas após a leitura dos textos. Observe:

Making inferences or inferring – A estratégia de inferência tem como objetivo fazê-lo capturar aquilo que não está dito no texto de forma explícita. Essas adivinhações podem ter como base as pistas dadas pelo próprio texto ou o seu próprio conhecimento. Trata-se de uma estratégia de leitura extremamente importante, pois um texto só terá sentido se você puder estabelecer relações entre as partes, ou seja, entre as palavras, frases, parágrafos etc.

Selecting a good title – Muitas vezes o título de um texto resume sua ideia central. Para selecionar o título mais apropriado para o texto que você acabou de ler, leia-o novamente e anote os pontos que mais chamaram sua atenção. O mesmo se aplica para quando você tiver que afirmar ou declarar a ideia ou o propósito principal do texto lido (*stating the main idea or the main purpose of the text*).

Understanding details – Para entender os detalhes de um texto é preciso fazer uma leitura lenta e concentrar-se durante essa leitura, isto é, ficar longe de qualquer coisa que possa distraí-lo. Recorrer a um dicionário para consultar as palavras e expressões desconhecidas e anotar seu significado, bem como fazer paráfrases durante a leitura, são algumas das ações que contribuem para a compreensão detalhada do texto. Podem contribuir, também, para as atividades que pedem que você resuma o texto lido (*summarizing*).

Understanding main ideas – Para realizar atividades que têm esta estratégia sinalizada, não é necessário fazer uma leitura tão detalhada, nem mesmo procurar todas as palavras desconhecidas em um dicionário. Basta fazer uma leitura geral do texto com atenção e compreender sua mensagem principal.

IRREGULAR VERBS

Base form	Past form	Past Participle	Translation
awake	awoke	awoken	acordar
be	was, were	been	ser, estar
become	became	become	tornar-se
begin	began	begun	começar
bend	bent	bent	dobrar
bet	bet	bet	apostar
bite	bit	bitten	morder
blow	blew	blown	soprar
break	broke	broken	quebrar
bring	brought	brought	trazer
build	built	built	construir
burn	burnt/burned	burnt/burned	queimar
buy	bought	bought	comprar
catch	caught	caught	pegar
choose	chose	chosen	escolher
come	came	come	vir
cut	cut	cut	cortar
do	did	done	fazer
draw	drew	drawn	desenhar
dream	dreamed/dreamt	dreamed/dreamt	sonhar
drink	drank	drunk	beber
drive	drove	driven	dirigir
eat	ate	eaten	comer
fall	fell	fallen	cair
feed	fed	fed	alimentar
feel	felt	felt	sentir
fight	fought	fought	lutar
find	found	found	achar
fly	flew	flown	voar
forget	forgot	forgotten	esquecer
forgive	forgave	forgiven	perdoar
get	got	got/gotten	conseguir
get up	got up	got up/gotten up	levantar-se
give	gave	given	dar
go	went	gone	ir
grow	grew	grown	crescer
hang out	hung out	hung out	passar tempo
have	had	had	ter
hear	heard	heard	ouvir
hide	hid	hidden	esconder
hit	hit	hit	atingir
hold	held	held	segurar
hurt	hurt	hurt	machucar
keep	kept	kept	manter

Base form	Past form	Past Participle	Translation
know	knew	known	saber, conhecer
lean	leant/leaned	leant/leaned	inclinar-se
learn	learnt/learned	learnt/learned	aprender
leave	left	left	deixar, sair
lend	lent	lent	emprestar
let	let	let	deixar
lose	lost	lost	perder
make	made	made	fazer
mean	meant	meant	significar
meet	met	met	encontrar, conhecer
overcome	overcame	overcome	superar
pay	paid	paid	pagar
put	put	put	colocar
read	read	read	ler
ride	rode	ridden	andar de
ring	rang	rung	tocar
rise	rose	risen	subir, aumentar
run	ran	run	correr
say	said	said	dizer
see	saw	seen	ver
sell	sold	sold	vender
send	sent	sent	enviar
set	set	set	estabelecer
show	showed	shown	mostrar
sing	sang	sung	cantar
sit	sat	sat	sentar
sleep	slept	slept	dormir
speak	spoke	spoken	falar
spell	spelled/spelt	spelled/spelt	soletrar
spend	spent	spent	gastar, passar tempo
split	split	split	dividir
stand up	stood up	stood up	ficar de pé
steal	stole	stolen	roubar
swim	swam	swum	nadar
take	took	taken	pegar, tomar
teach	taught	taught	ensinar
tell	told	told	contar
think	thought	thought	pensar
throw	threw	thrown	jogar
understand	understood	understood	entender
wake up	woke up	woken up	acordar
wear	wore	worn	vestir
win	won	won	ganhar
write	wrote	written	escrever

COMMON MISTAKES

Speakers of Portuguese are more likely to make certain mistakes in English because of interference from Portuguese. Let's take a look at some common mistakes:

TOPIC	COMMON MISTAKE	RIGHT FORM	SOME EXPLANATION
SAYING ONE'S AGE	I ~~have~~ sixteen years old.	I <u>am</u> sixteen years old.	In Portuguese, we use the verb *have* for saying one's age, but in English we use the verb *be*.
ASKING QUESTIONS	You study geography with Mr. Perry?	"<u>Do</u> you study geography with Mr. Perry?	In Portuguese, we ask questions changing the intonation of the sentence. The same does not work in English as we need an auxiliary to form questions.
USING -S FOR THIRD PERSON SINGULAR IN THE SIMPLE PRESENT	My little sister always ~~complain~~ when I can't give her attention.	My little sister always <u>complains</u> when I can't give her attention.	It may be confusing to use -s at the end of verbs for the third person singular when we immediately associate the -s with plural. Beware! The -s in this case is <u>not</u> plural, it is just the correct verb form.
YOUR vs. HIS/HER	Laura is very cute, ~~your~~ voice is sweet, and ~~your~~ smile is beautiful.	Laura is very cute, <u>her</u> voice is sweet, and <u>her</u> smile is beautiful.	Translating *your (seu/sua/seus/suas)* may be tricky because in Portuguese we say, for example: "Laura é muito fofa, <u>sua</u> voz é doce e <u>seu</u> sorriso largo". However, in this case we do not use *your voice* or *your smile*, we have to think of "voz dela", "sorriso dela".
NEGATIVE ORDERS AND INSTRUCTIONS	~~No~~ touch!	Don't touch!	In Portuguese, when we give negative orders or instructions we say, for example: "Não toque!" However, in English we need the auxiliary.
TALKING ABOUT POSSESSIONS	The house of John is huge!	John's house is huge!	In Portuguese, we do not have the use of 's for possessions because we usually use the possession before the person. In English, it is the opposite, so we use 's to identify that something belongs to someone else.
IRREGULAR PLURAL	More people ~~is~~ arriving soon.	More people are arriving soon.	Because irregular plural words do not always end with an -s, it can easily be mistaken with a singular word, but we need to use a plural verb.
HAVE vs. THERE + BE	~~Have~~ a spider on the wall.	There is a spider on the wall.	When we use "ter" meaning "haver/existir", we can't use *have*. We need to use *there + be*.

FALSE FRIENDS

False friends are words with similar sound and form, but with different meanings. When we look at the word *actually*, for example, we immediately associate it with the Portuguese word "*atualmente*", because of its similarity. However, *actually* means "*na realidade*" as in "It **actually** costs three thousand dollars, not three hundred." Let's take a look at some other examples.

English	Portuguese translation	Example	Don't get confused with...	Which in English is...
alias	pseudônimo, nome falso	He used to work under an **alias**.	aliás	by the way
anthem	hino	Are you able to sing the American national **anthem**?	antena	antenna
appoint	nomear	Tom Leary was **appointed** to a new position.	apontar	point
assist	ajudar	Who is going to **assist** the new judge?	assistir	watch
college	faculdade	I can't believe you are not excited about going to **college**!	colégio	school
comprehensive	abrangente, amplo	It was a very **comprehensive** report.	compreensível	understandable
convict	condenado(a)	The **convict** had to be handcuffed.	convicto(a)	certain
costume	fantasia	How much is the vampire **costume**?	costume	habit
data	dados	We have gathered a lot of **data** on the subject.	data	date
exit	saída	Where is the **exit** door?	êxito	success
fabric	tecido	Silk is a very expensive **fabric**.	fábrica	factory
hazard	risco	This medicine presents no **hazard** to your health.	azar	bad luck
inhabited	habitado(a)	It is an **inhabited** island.	inabitado(a)	uninhabited
journal	revista especializada, diário	Tom is the editor of a very important medical **journal**.	jornal	newspaper
lecture	palestra	The **lecture** had a very young audience.	leitura	reading
legend	lenda	Have you heard of the **legend** of Billy Jack?	legenda	subtitle
library	biblioteca	Is there a **library** around here where I can borrow some comics?	livraria	bookstore
novel	romance	*My Brilliant Friend* is a **novel** written by Elena Ferrante, a mysterious Italian writer.	novela	soap opera
notice	notar, observar	Have you **noticed** the new furniture in the study hall?	notícia	news
parents	pais	My **parents** got married in the early nineties.	parentes	relatives
physician	médico	He is a respected **physician** who is looking after the president's health.	físico	physicist
prejudice	preconceito	We must always fight against all kinds of **prejudice**.	prejuízo	harm
pretend	fingir	Stop **pretending**! I know you are not telling the truth.	pretender	intend
realize	perceber	Have you **realized** how far we are from our goal?	realizar	accomplish
resume	recomeçar	After a long break they **resumed** the session.	resumir	summarize
sensible	sensato(a)	Choosing to cross the river in such a small boat is not a **sensible** option.	sensível	sensitive
support	apoiar	The homeless shelter is **supported** by a group of volunteers.	suportar	bear

97

GLOSSARY

Unit 1

blending – mescla
desirability – desejabilidade
knowledge – conhecimento
retire – aposentar-se
settle – estabelecer-se
status quo – situação atual (latim)

Unit 2

agreeable – colaborativo (para uma pessoa)
approach – abordagem
baked – assado(a)
blood pressure – pressão sanguínea
bowel – intestino
canned – enlatado(a)
cantaloupe – melão-cantalupe
celery – aipo
cucumbers – pepinos
cut-up – cortado(a)
dried apricots – damascos secos
folate – folato, um tipo de vitamina B
growth – crescimento
halibut – peixe linguado
ingrained – enraizado
iron – ferro
lays out – dispõe (infinitivo: *lay out*)
likewise – da mesma forma
lower intake – baixo consumo
moon fruit – araçá-boi
mushrooms – cogumelos
outcomes – resultados
pleasing – agradável
pureed – pure

raw – cru
released – lançou (infinitivo: *release*)
rendering – representar (infinitivo: *render*)
sauces – molhos
set the tone – dar o tom
source – fonte
soy beans – soja
squash – abobrinha
star fruit – carambola
stir-fry – refogar
strengthening – fortalecer (infinitivo: *strengthen*)
tissues – tecidos
tuna – atum
white beans – feijões brancos

Review 1

behave – comportar-se
cutlery – cutelaria
matters – importa (infinitivo: *matter*)
obfuscated – ofuscado(a)
sky-rocketed – disparou (infinitivo: *sky-rocket*)
spiraling – rotativo(a)
tuck into – cair dentro

Unit 3

embolden – encorajar
harass – assediar
provide – oferecer
raw – puro, cru
shelf life – vida útil
strengthen – fortalecer
toward – em direção a

Unit 4

caregivers – cuidadores
downside – lado negativo
peer – igual
release – liberação
soothed – acalmado (infinitivo: *soothe*)
trigger – provocar

Review 2

accountability – prestação de contas
hazard – risco
scholarship – bolsa de estudos
undoubtedly – sem sombra de dúvida, indubitavelmente
unfairly – injustamente
witnessed – presenciamos (infinitivo: *witness*)
zealously – zelosamente, com cuidado

Unit 5

coiffure – cabeleireiro
enhance – aumentar
buried – enterrado (infinitvo: *burry*)
heightened – maior
laundromat – lavanderia automática
realm – reino
seeks – busca (infinitivo: *seek*)
sheeting – película
summit – cúpula, reunião de líderes
swapping – trocando (infinitivo: *swap*)

Unit 6

afford – proporcionar
apparel – vestimenta

appeal – agrado
fulfills – cumpre (infinitivo: *fulfill*)
guilty – culpado(a)
hubbas – oba!
prosecutors – promotores
raided – deu uma batida (policial)
remain – permanecer
scholarships – bolsas de estudos
seemingly – aparentemente
sizzling – quente, acalorado
sponsors – patrocinadores
staging – organizar, apresentar (infinitivo: *stage*)
stormed out – saiu irado(a) (infinitivo: *storm out*)
submitted – enviou (infinitivo: *submit*)
turf – relva, gramado
venues – locais
wielding – exercendo
youth – juventude

Review 3

expertly – habilmente
grasp – segurar
though – mas, apesar disso

Unit 7

beyond – além
boardroom – sala de reunião
broadcaster – locutor
claiming – alegando (infinitivo: *claim*)
contenders – competidores
cravat – peitilho (gravata)
dashing – elegante
deeds – atos, ações

GLOSSARY

erstwhile – antigo

forecasting – previsão

patois – dialeto, gíria

pidgin – simplificado

purposes – propósitos

put the kibosh on – destruir uma ideia

researcher – pesquisador

shifts – muda (infinitivo: *shift*)

spreading – espalhando-se

struggle – esforçar-se, ter dificuldade

takes stock of – avalia algo (infinitivo: *take stock of*)

turnout – comparecimento

whether – se

witty – sagaz

Unit 8

accounts – justifica (infinitivo: *account*)

beating – batida

belongings – pertences

bundle – embrulho

bursting – repentinamente e com impulso

chap – amigo

double-barreled – duplo

dual-purpose – com propósito duplo

flair – talento

grunting – grunhindo

hamper – cesto

likens – assemelha-se (infinitivo: *liken*)

mosque – mesquita

ounce – medida correspondente a 28,34 gramas

pouring – servindo

proponent – proponente, defensor

remained – permaneceu (infinitivo: *remain*)

restless – inquieto(a)

sought – buscou (infinitivo: *seek*)

strapped – quebrado(a)

striking – impressionante

wardrobe – guarda-roupa

wish – desejar

Review 4

beyond doubt – sem sombra de dúvida

boost – estimular

hitherto – até este ponto

lag – atraso

launch – lançamento

neatly – organizadamente

outpacing – ultrapassando (infinitivo: *outpace*)

pecking order – hierarquia

reckons – estima (infinitivo: *reckon*)

widespread – difundido(a)

NOTES

NOTES

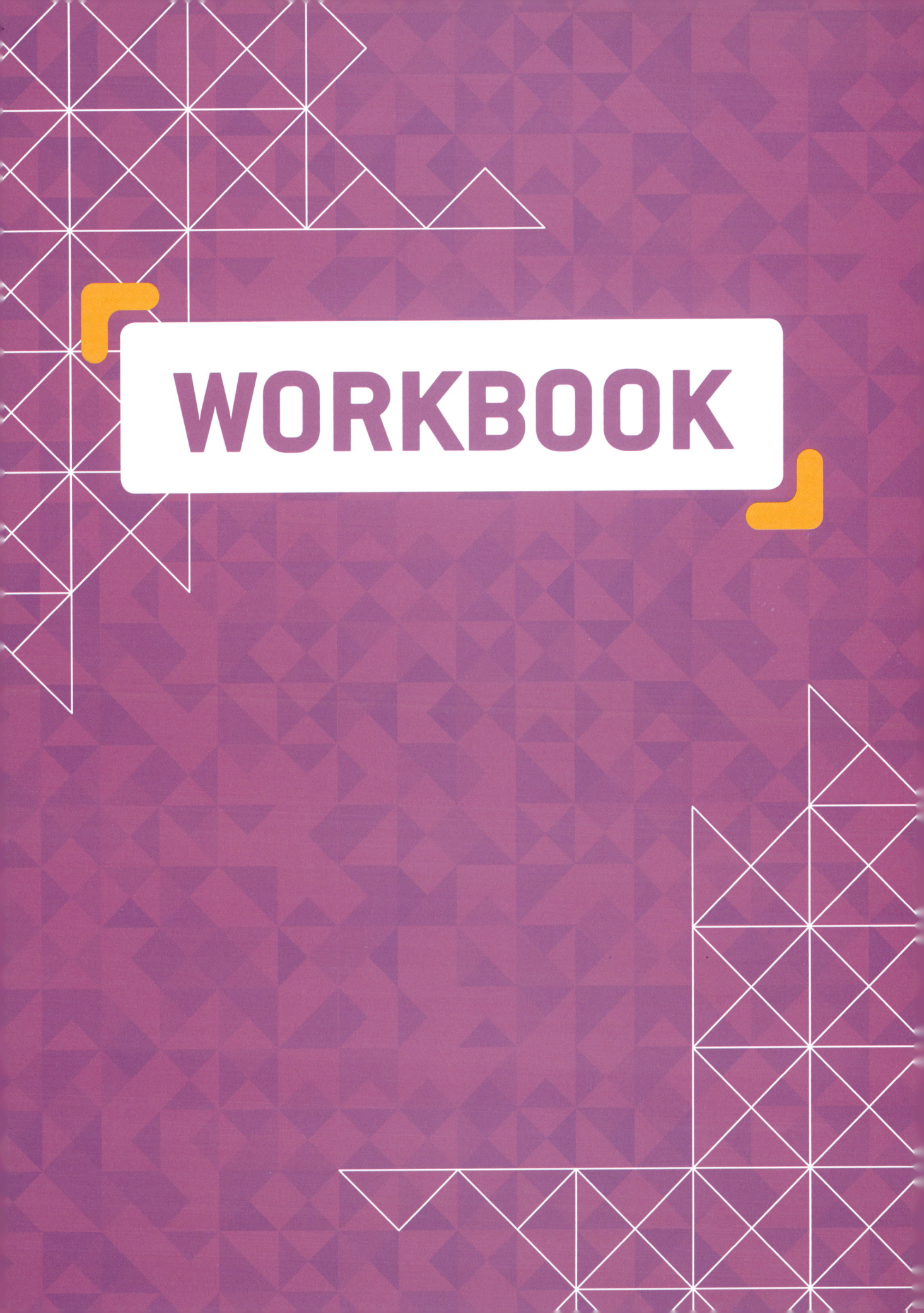

WORKBOOK

Unit 1 — Migration Trends

1. Look at the bar chart extracted from the UN's International Migration Report 2017 and find information to complete the sentences below. **Scanning**

   a. The chart compares migration in the years _____ and _____.

   b. The country which had the largest number of migrants in both years was _____.

   c. In 2000, Canada hosted _____ million international migrants.

   d. In 2017, the United Kingdom hosted _____ million international migrants.

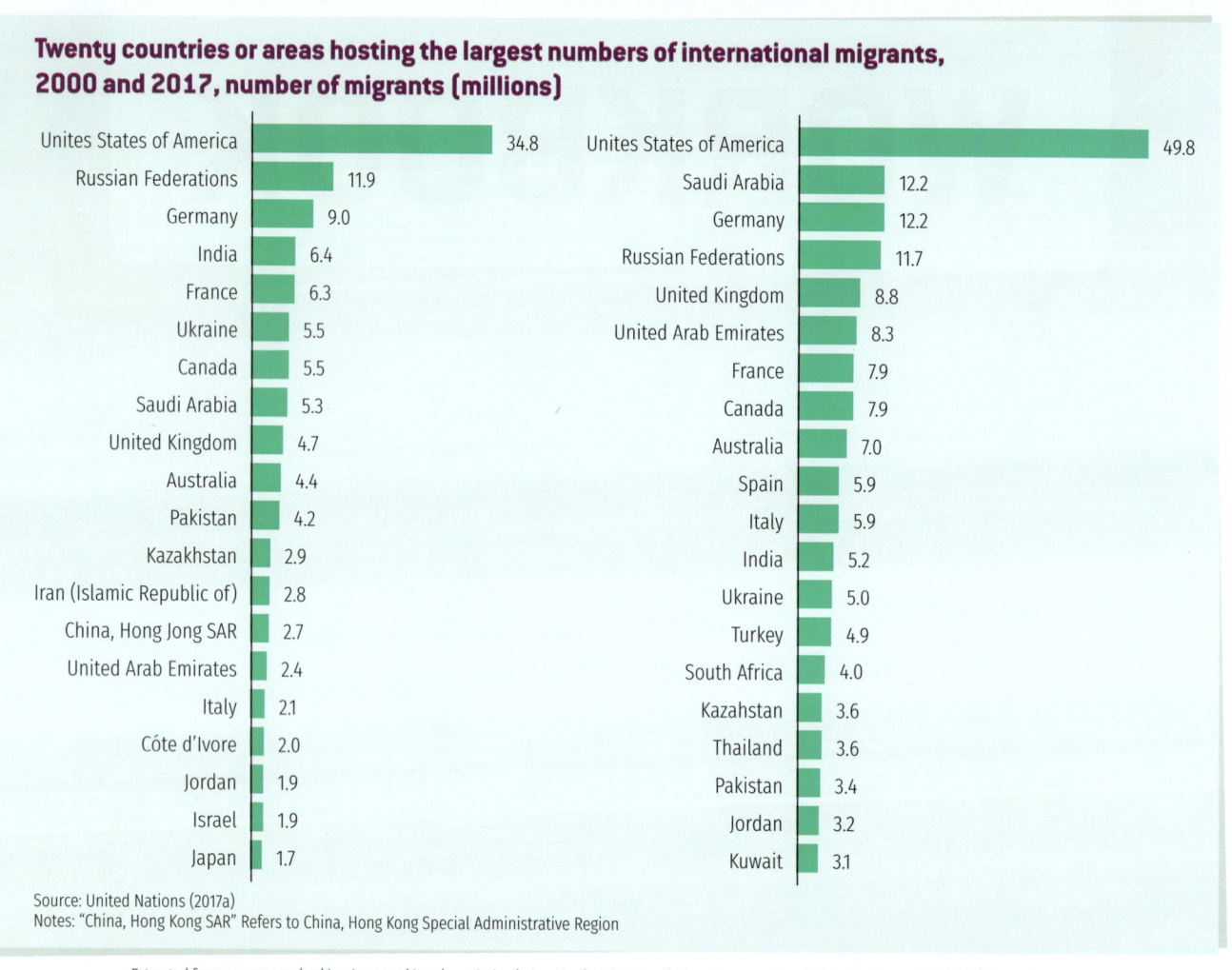

   Twenty countries or areas hosting the largest numbers of international migrants, 2000 and 2017, number of migrants (millions)

2000		2017	
Unites States of America	34.8	Unites States of America	49.8
Russian Federations	11.9	Saudi Arabia	12.2
Germany	9.0	Germany	12.2
India	6.4	Russian Federations	11.7
France	6.3	United Kingdom	8.8
Ukraine	5.5	United Arab Emirates	8.3
Canada	5.5	France	7.9
Saudi Arabia	5.3	Canada	7.9
United Kingdom	4.7	Australia	7.0
Australia	4.4	Spain	5.9
Pakistan	4.2	Italy	5.9
Kazakhstan	2.9	India	5.2
Iran (Islamic Republic of)	2.8	Ukraine	5.0
China, Hong Jong SAR	2.7	Turkey	4.9
United Arab Emirates	2.4	South Africa	4.0
Italy	2.1	Kazahstan	3.6
Côte d'Ivore	2.0	Thailand	3.6
Jordan	1.9	Pakistan	3.4
Israel	1.9	Jordan	3.2
Japan	1.7	Kuwait	3.1

   Source: United Nations (2017a)
   Notes: "China, Hong Kong SAR" Refers to China, Hong Kong Special Administrative Region

   Extracted from www.un.org/en/development/desa/population/migration/publications/migrationreport/docs/MigrationReport2017_Highlights.pdf. Accessed on May 25, 2018.

2. Complete these excerpts with the verb *be* in the affirmative or negative form.

   a. "Immigration _____ the international movement of people into a destination country of which they are not natives [...]"

   Extracted from www.wikipedia.org/wiki/Immigration. Accessed on March 10, 2018.

   b. "[...] As for economic effects, research suggests that migration _____ beneficial both to the receiving and sending countries. [...]"

   Extracted from www.wikipedia.org/wiki/Immigration. Accessed on March 10, 2018.

   c. Launched in May 2016, *I _____ a refugee* is a digital platform that intends to humanize the discussions about refugees; to allow refugees to speak for themselves; and to fight growing populism, fears, stereotypes, and prejudice.

   Adapted from www.workshopx.org/im-not-refugee. Accessed on March 10, 2018.

3. **Unscramble the words and write questions. Then match the questions with the answers.**

   a. the purpose / of your visit / is / business / ?
   _____

   b. here alone / are / you / ?
   _____

   c. these / your bags / are / ?
   _____

   d. a problem / migration / to another / from one country / is / ?
   _____

   e. migration / immigration / is / the same as / ?
   _____

   f. they / from / China / are / ?
   _____

   (   ) No, they are different. Immigration means entering another country to live permanently.
   (   ) There are pros and cons. I cannot say it is a real problem.
   (   ) No. Those are my bags over there.
   (   ) Yes, they are. They're from Hong Kong.
   (   ) No, my wife and daughters are with me.
   (   ) No, I'm here on vacation.

4. **Use the correct form of the verbs in the box to complete the following texts.**

   > happen   be (x2)   occur   spread

   a. Cultural diffusion _____ via human migration, intercultural marriages, or cultural exchange via letters, books, or electronic media. It _____ a phenomenon in which specific cultural concepts, ideas, or technologies _____ from one culture to another.

   Adapted from www.answers.com/Q/Does_migration_cause_cultural_diffusion. Accessed on March 10, 2018.

   b. In a very simple definition, cultural diffusion is when different cultures are spread into different areas. It _____ the mixing or **blending** of different ideas, beliefs, and innovations from one group to another. Cultural diffusion _____ all over the world, from fast food restaurants to new technologies.

   Adapted from http://bookbuilder.cast.org/view_print.php?book=63595. Accessed on March 10, 2018.

5. **Transform these statements into negatives.**

   a. Cultural diffusion always leads to positive exchanges.
   _____

   b. Immigration plays an important role in cultural diffusion.
   _____

   c. Most refugees seek asylum in other countries.
   _____

6. Match the questions with the answers.
   a. How does the Internet affect cultural diffusion in the world today?
   b. What does cultural diffusion mean?
   c. How does globalization lead to cultural exchange?
   ( ) Globalization provides both positive and negative influences on cultural diversity.
   ( ) The effect that it has on both local and global cultures is significant.
   ( ) The spreading out of culture, culture traits, or a cultural pattern from a central point.

7. Look at the ads closely. Then use one of the imperative statements below to complete each message.

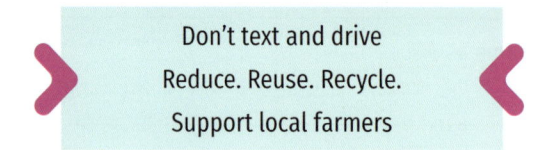

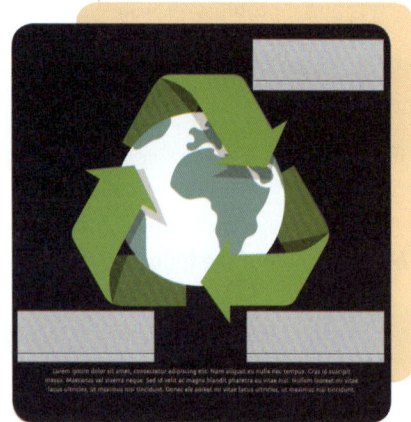

> Don't text and drive
> Reduce. Reuse. Recycle.
> Support local farmers

8. Form adjectives with the suffixes from the box. Then use the adjectives to complete the sentences below.

> -ful   -ive   -ous   -able / -ible   -less   -al

a. use _____
b. color _____
c. comfort _____
d. danger _____
e. mathematics _____
f. attract _____

1. I love her new blouse; it's so _____ .
2. Wear _____ shoes to walk around the city.
3. They usually record changes with _____ precision.
4. Don't text and drive because it's _____ .
5. These old cell phones are _____ ; they can't be updated.
6. I don't think he's _____ .

9. Complete the sentences with the correct word from the box.

> drought   employment
> flooding   hazards

a. Some push factors for immigration are natural _____ such as _____ or _____.

b. Some people also migrate to look for better _____ opportunities.

AN EYE ON ENEM

ENEM 2012 – Prova Amarela
Questão 92

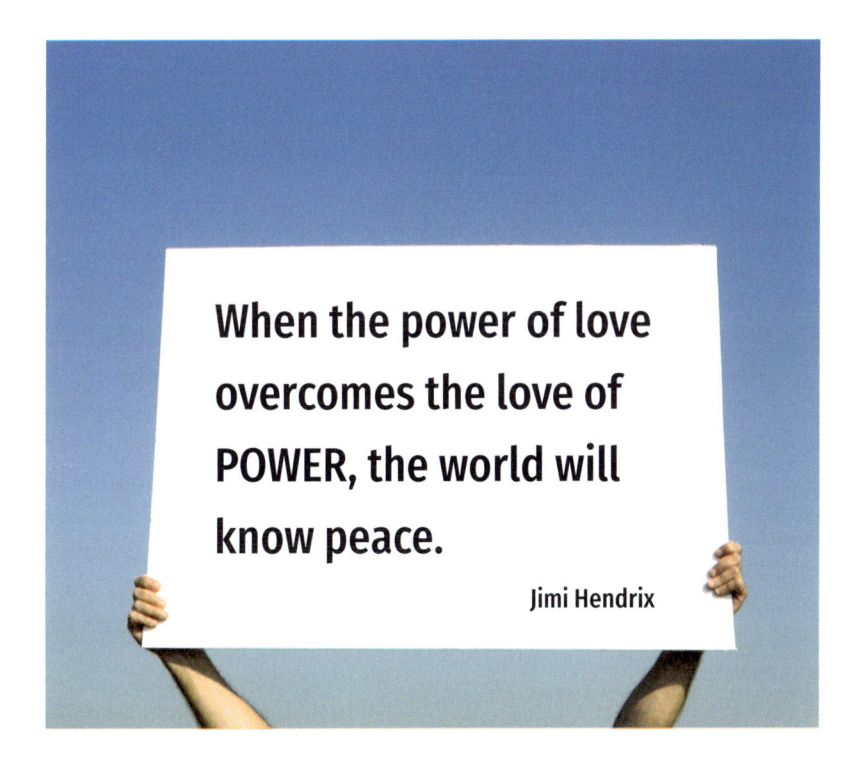

> When the power of love overcomes the love of POWER, the world will know peace.
>
> Jimi Hendrix

Aproveitando-se de seu status social e da possível influência sobre seus fãs, o famoso músico Jimi Hendrix associa, em seu texto, os termos *love*, *power* e *peace* para justificar sua opinião de que

a. a paz tem o poder de aumentar o amor entre os homens.

b. o amor pelo poder deve ser menor do que o poder do amor.

c. o poder deve ser compartilhado entre aqueles que se amam.

d. o amor pelo poder é capaz de desunir cada vez mais as pessoas.

e. a paz será alcançada quando a busca pelo poder deixar de existir.

Unit 2 — "The First Wealth is Health"

1. **Read the text and choose the best title for it.** *Skimming*
   a. Nutritional guidelines around the world. ( )
   b. Brazil has the best nutritional guidelines in the world. ( )
   c. Brazil and the USA have the same nutritional guidelines. ( )

> The way we talk about nutrition in this country is absurd. And you only need to look as far as Brazil to understand why.
>
> Yesterday, a U.S. government-appointed scientific panel **released** a 600-page report that will inform America's new dietary guidelines. These guidelines only come out every five years, and they matter because they truly **set the tone** for how Americans eat. […]
>
> But this panel and their guidelines too often over complicate what we know about healthy eating. They take a rather punitive **approach** to food, reducing it to its nutrient parts and emphasizing its relationship to obesity. […]
>
> To fully understand the absurdity of the food situation in America, let's turn back to Brazil. Brazil is clearly a very different context than America. The country has only relatively recently emerged as a global economic force, and under-nutrition is still as much a concern as the rising obesity problem. But it's a fascinating country when it comes to health and it's probably exactly their emerging status that has forced them to be smarter about food and nutrition.
>
> In 143 pages, the Brazilian health ministry also **lays out** what may be the most intelligent food guide in the world. Here are some highlights from an English translation:
>
> **On whole foods:** "Make natural or minimally processed foods the basis of your diet. Natural or minimally processed foods, in great variety, mainly of plant origin, are the basis for diets that are nutritious, delicious, appropriate, and supportive of socially and environmentally sustainable food systems."
>
> **On salt, sugar and fat:** "Use oils, fats, salt, and sugar in small amounts for seasoning and cooking foods and to create culinary preparations. As long as they are used in moderation in culinary preparations based on natural or minimally processed foods, oils, fats, salt, and sugar contribute toward diverse and delicious diets without **rendering** them nutritionally unbalanced."
>
> **On processed foods:** "Because of their ingredients, ultra-processed foods—such as packaged snacks, soft drinks, and instant noodles—are nutritionally unbalanced. Ultra-processed foods are formulated and packaged to be ready-to-consume without any preparation. This makes meals and sharing of food at table unnecessary."
>
> **On eating as a social experience:** "Clean, quiet, and comfortable places encourage attention to the act of eating mindfully and slowly, enable meals to be fully appreciated, and decrease overeating… Humans are social beings. Eating together is **ingrained** in human history, as is the sharing and division of responsibility for finding, acquiring, preparing, and cooking food. Eating together is a natural, simple yet profound way to create and develop relationships between people. Thus, eating is a natural part of social life."
>
> Adapted from www.vox.com/2015/2/20/8076961/brazil-food-guide. Accessed on June 25, 2018.

2. **Number the recommendations 1-4 as they are mentioned in the text.** *Understanding details*
   a. Use oils, fats, salt, and sugar in small amounts for seasoning and cooking. ( )
   b. Eating together helps to develop relationships with people. ( )
   c. Avoid processed and ultra-processed foods. ( )
   d. Make natural or minimally processed foods the basis of your diet. ( )

3. Below are photos of lunches that follow the Brazilian dietary guidelines. Complete the captions with the food items that are missing.

a. Rice, beans, baked _____ leg, beetroot, and cornmeal with _____ .

b. Rice, _____, omelette, and sautéed jilo.

c. Feijoada, _____, onion and tomato vinaigrette, cassava flower, sautéed cole, and _____ .

d. _____ salad, rice, beans, grilled beef, and fruit salad.

Source: Brazilian Dietary Guidelines. www.foodpolitics.com/wp-content/uploads/Brazilian-Dietary-Guidelines-2014.pdf. Accessed on June 26, 2018.

4. Complete the table with words from the previous activity.

Fruits and vegetables	Proteins	Grains	Dairy

5. Complete the following sentences using the simple present form of the verbs in paretheses.

a. Riley usually _____ (prefer) places that serve freshly-made meals.

b. The quality of fruit and vegetables that Steve _____ (buy) in supermarkets is not as good as at farms.

c. _____ you _____ (eat) fresh fruit and vegetables every day?

d. I _____ (not pay) attention to the type of milk I use; should I?

e. Susan _____ (not have) lunch at home, so she _____ (try) to have healthy snacks with her.

109

6. Rewrite the sentences to include the adverb in parentheses in the correct place.

   a. In Brazil, cow's milk is consumed with fruit or with coffee at the first meal of the day. (often)
   _____

   b. People think that it costs a lot to eat healthily. (often)
   _____

   c. Animal foods are good sources of proteins, vitamins, and minerals. (usually)
   _____

   d. I eat junk. It doesn't make me feel good. (rarely)
   _____

   e. Fresh fruit and vegetables are better for your health than processed foods. (always)
   _____

   f. People comment on my green drinks, but I love them! (always)
   _____

7. Choose the best option to complete each sentence.

   1. A processed food is _____ easily recognizable as a modified version of the original food.

   a. frequently   **b.** never   **c.** usually   **d.** daily

   2. _____ choose natural or minimally processed foods and freshly made dishes and meals over ultra-processed foods.

   a. Often   **b.** Always   **c.** Sometimes   **d.** Rarely

   3. Far too often, people go on extreme diets they can't maintain, which means they _____ actually develop long-term, healthy eating habits.

   a. always   **b.** sometimes   **c.** never   **d.** often

   4. _____ people need to accept and act on the fact that food, diet, and nutrition are vital to their health, and also to the health of others in their lives.

   a. Never   **b.** Sometimes   **c.** Frequently   **d.** Regularly

8. Rewrite the sentences replacing the words in bold with the correct subject or object pronoun.

   a. Susan borrowed some of my books, but **Susan** returned **the books** yesterday.
   _____

   b. Look at Rodrigo's new shoes! **The shoes** look very nice on **Rodrigo**.
   _____

   c. The Brazilian Dietary Guidelines state that oil, salt, and sugar should be used in moderation. **Oil, salt, and sugar** can be harmful when consumed in large amounts.
   _____

   d. My classmates and I love our cooking classes with Mr. Simmons. **Mr. Simmons** teaches **my classmates and me** a lot of new recipes.
   _____

9. Complete the article with the words from the box.

> habits consume have intakes important
> fat vegetables is (x2) breakfast gain

Breakfast eating among Brazilian adolescents: Analysis of the National Dietary Survey 2008-2009

Eating habits _____ a significant influence on the growth, development, and health of individuals. High consumption of _____ and sugar-rich foods and low consumption of fruit and _____ has been observed among Brazilian adolescents, resulting in nutritionally inadequate diets. Meal skipping and eating away from home have also been observed. Moreover, when compared to adults and older adults, Brazilian adolescents _____ more soft drinks, cookies, and sandwiches and fewer beans, salads, and vegetables.

Breakfast _____ considered the first and most _____ meal of the day. The quality of food at breakfast has been identified as essential for children and adolescents to achieve or maintain adequate health conditions since the consumption of cereal and fruit _____ important for the prevention of chronic non-communicable diseases. In children and adolescents, _____ has been associated with improvement in attention, memory, and mood; it has also been possibly associated with improvements in motivation, cognitive function, and academic achievement, as well as with higher _____ of vitamin D and calcium. However, irregular breakfast _____ have been associated with unfavorable health outcomes and weight _____ among adolescents.

Adapted from www.scielo.br/scielo.php?script=sci_arttext&pid=S1415-52732017000400463. Accessed on June 26, 2018.

AN EYE ON ENEM

ENEM 2016 – Prova Azul

Questão 95

BOGOF (buy one, get one free) is used as a noun in 'There are some great bogofs on at the supermarket' or as an adjective, usually with a word such as offer or deal – 'there are some great bogof offers in store'.

When you combine the first letters of the words in a phrase or the name of an organization, you have an acronym. Acronyms are spoken as a word so NATO (North Atlantic Treaty Organization) is not pronounced N-A-T-O. We say NATO. Bogof, when said outloud, is quite comical for a native speaker, as it sounds like an insult. 'Bog off!' meaning go away, leave me alone, is slightly childish and a little old-fashioned.

BOGOF is the best-known of the supermarket marketing strategies. The concept was first imported from the USA during the 1970s recession, when food prices were very high. It came back into fashion in the late 1990s, led by big supermarket chains trying to gain a competitive advantage over each other. Consumers were attracted by the idea that they could get something for nothing. Who could possibly say 'no'?

Disponível em: www.bbc.co.uk. Acesso em: 2 ago. 2012 (adaptado).

Considerando-se as informações do texto, a expressão "bogof" é usada para

a. anunciar mercadorias em promoção.
b. pedir para uma pessoa se retirar.
c. comprar produtos fora de moda.
d. indicar recessão na economia.
e. chamar alguém em voz alta.

Unit 3 — Your Digital Self

1. **Look at the information below, extracted from research published in *The Guardian*, and complete the statements.** *Scanning*
   a. The number of people in the UK between the ages of 18 and 24 expected to stop using Facebook in 2018 is _____.
   b. As of 2017, most Facebook users in the UK are between the ages of _____ and _____.
   c. The number of people in the UK between the ages of 55 and 64 expected to join Facebook in 2018 is _____.
   d. As of 2017, 2.2 million Facebook users in the UK are between the ages of _____ and _____.

   > **Is Facebook for old people? Over-55s flock in as the young leave**
   > Facebook UK users 2017 vs. 2018
   > **Age 12 to 17** 2.2m, down 300,000
   > **Age 18 to 24** 4.5, down 400,000
   > **Age 25 to 34** 7.2m, flat
   > **Age 35 to 44** 5.9m, flat
   > **Age 45 to 54** 5.6m, up 100,000 users
   > **Age 55 to 64** 3.5m, up 200,000 users
   > **Age 65-plus** 2.9m, up 300,000 users
   >
   > Extracted from www.theguardian.com/technology/2018/feb/12/is-facebook-for-old-people-over-55s-flock-in-as-the-young-leave. Accessed on June 17, 2018.

2. **Complete the sentences with the correct possessive adjective.**
   a. Jason is always on _____ phone posting pictures of himself and _____ friends. Jason's friends also love posting pictures on _____ social networks – they even have a group only for that.
   b. This is _____ sister Maria. She is 5 years older than me, but we get along very well. We like to ride _____ bikes at the park in the afternoon when it's cool.
   c. Can I use _____ phone? _____ phone's battery is dead.
   d. Is this _____ backpack? Someone left it in the schoolyard.
   e. Brazil is famous for _____ beaches, but it should be famous for all _____ natural beauties.
   f. Tina forgot _____ jacket, can you return it to her?

3. **Match the false friends in the sentences below with their meanings.**
   a. Actually, I'm not afraid of traveling alone.
   b. Have you seen Bob lately?
   c. What is the most durable fabric for clothing?
   d. I work in a factory that manufactures decorative accessories.

   (   ) cloth produced especially by knitting, weaving, or felting fibers

   (   ) in fact, in reality

   (   ) not long ago, recently

   (   ) a building or group of buildings in which goods are manufactured

4. Fill in the blanks using the false friends from the box.

> newspapers   lately   actually   fabric   journal   factory

a. This _____ is very chic. It's made of cotton with details in silk.

b. Some people use Facebook as a personal _____ .

c. I haven't seen any of my friends _____ .

d. He is the HR manager at the _____ .

e. I don't buy _____ I read the news online.

f. This letter is _____ for you, not for me.

5. Underline the false friends in the excerpts below. Then underline the alternative that best summarizes the paragraph.

1.

> Social media platforms have become a dominant source of data used by governments, corporations, and academics to study human society. Yet, in the rush **towards** ever-more sophisticated algorithms and visualizations to analyze trends from social media, we are ignoring the critical questions of how well social media actually reflects societal trends and just how to use all of the analysis we produce.
>
> Extracted from www.forbes.com/sites/kalevleetaru/2016/02/16/does-social-media-actually-reflect-reality/#61e292cf4e43. Accessed on June 18, 2018.

a. Social media is an accurate data source for social trends.

b. Social trends are usually followed and displayed in social media, as research continues to demonstrate.

c. Social media never reflects social trends; therefore, one is not related to the other.

d. It's still uncertain how social media and social trends are related. One doesn't necessarily reflect the other.

e. The more people use social media, the more information will be accurate.

2.

> If kids are online, parents are usually more effective acting as mentors than as micromanagers. Having open-ended conversations rather than wielding authoritative control enables kids to build the critical-thinking skills needed to make smarter decisions online and in real life. For some kids, a finsta ("fake" Instagram) or a rinsta ("real" Instagram) might be where they feel they can share their **raw**, authentic feelings, even though they don't always realize that anything shared online has the potential for a greater audience, amplified consequences or longer **shelf life**. It's up to parents to find a way in, not through coercion, but through conversation.
>
> Extracted from www.washingtonpost.com/news/parenting/wp/2018/01/09/what-teens-wish-their-parents-knew-about-social-media/?noredirect=on&utm_term=.017d8dc1dead. Accessed on June 19, 2018.

a. Parents should keep track of their kids' life on social media in order to control their online interactions.

b. Micromanaging is important once children start hiding their online activities from their parents.

c. Critical-thinking skills are built on imposition and by modeling behavior with punishment.

d. Understanding how kids interact through social media involves micromanaging and authoritative control.

e. When dealing with kids, offering good advice and mentoring is usually more effective than being imposing and dictatorial.

6. Complete the sentences with the correct form of the verbs in the box.

> be   think   decide   help   spend

a. Kids usually _____ most of their time on social media and online games rather than studying or having face-to-face interactions.

b. Most parents _____ small children shouldn't be allowed to go online without supervision, because they might be exposed to harm and danger.

c. Teenagers _____ getting more and more resourceful as time goes by. They can solve most types of problems without asking their parents for support.

d. Children shouldn't be allowed to _____ how much time they spend on social media. Parents' supervision is important to help them develop awareness.

e. Cyberbullying is real, and parents must act as mentors and _____ kids navigate through social media the safest way possible.

7. Read the sentences below and note the verbs in bold. Then match them with their meaning.

a. Anthony **looks down on** anyone who doesn't have a Master's degree.

b. Sonja **looks after** her sister whenever their parents are out.

c. I've always **looked up to** my grandfather. He's accomplished a lot in his life.

d. The detectives are **looking into** the crime, but there are no suspects yet.

(   ) to respect something or someone, and to show respect

(   ) to try to find out information

(   ) to take care of something or someone

(   ) to not value something or someone

8. Fill in the blanks with the verbs in the box.

> look up to   look after   look into   look down on

a. "See, there's a difference between you and me. You _____ people because of what YOU THINK they can or can't afford. You clearly believe that a man's worth should be measured by the car he chooses to drive… but I think differently."

Adapted from www.pmnewsnigeria.com/2018/07/18/banky-w-replies-ladies-trolling-him/. Acessed on July 19, 2018.

b. "Danica Patrick, the first woman to win an IndyCar race, had simple advice for people who _____ her: know what you love."

Extracted from www.abc11.com/sports/danica-patrick-makes-espys-history-as-first-female-host/3777902/. Acessed on July 19, 2018.

c. "This means you have to keep in mind that there are loads of things that potentially pose a risk to your children. The more you can do to address these problems, the better the kids will be as a result. So, these are some of the best ideas you can come up with that are going to help you _____ your kids' well-being right now!"

Extracted from www.t2conline.com/look-after-your-kids-well-being-with-these-great-parenting-ideas/. Acessed on July 19, 2018.

d. "Two US senators, members of the Commerce, Science, and Transportation Committee, have asked the Federal Trade Commission (FTC) to _____ the private policies and practices of smart TV manufacturers."

Extracted from www.telecompaper.com/news/us-senators-call-on-ftc-to-look-into-smart-tv-privacy-practices--1252840. Acessed on July 19, 2018.

Unit 3

9. Choose the correct option to complete the sentences below.

a. _____ Tony _____ a message now?
   a. Does / write
   b. Is / writing

b. Jude and Tom _____ their children anymore. They usually communicate through social media.
   a. don't call
   b. are not calling

c. We sometimes _____ to the movies together.
   a. go
   b. are going

d. First, I _____ dinner then I _____ my emails.
   a. have / read
   b. am having / am reading

10. Fill in the blanks with the simple present or the present continuous using the information given.

a. Peter _____ (not like) playing soccer with his siblings.

b. _____ you _____ (call) your mother now?

c. _____ they _____ (go) to the same restaurant every week?

d. Mark _____ (not eat) meat. He's a vegetarian.

e. George and Peter _____ (walk) to the park every Sunday morning.

f. Sue _____ (not be) now. She _____ (watch) TV.

AN EYE ON ENEM

ENEM 2013 – Prova Cinza
Questão 93

STEVE JOBS: A LIFE REMEMBERED 1955-2011

Readersdigest.ca takes a look back at Steve Jobs, and his contribution to our digital world.

CEO. Tech-Guru. Artist. There are few corporate figures as famous and well regarded as former Apple CEO, Steve Jobs. His list of achievements is staggering, and his contribution to modern technology, digital media, and indeed the world as a whole, cannot be downplayed.

With his passing on October 5, 2011, readersdigest.ca looks back at some of his greatest achievements, and pays our respects to a digital pioneer who helped pave the way for a generation of technology and possibilities, few could have imagined.

Disponível em www.readersdigest.ca. Acesso em: 25 fev. 2012.

Informações sobre pessoas famosas são recorrentes na mídia, divulgadas de forma impressa ou virtualmente. Em relação a Steve Jobs, este texto propõe:

a. Expor as maiores conquistas da empresa.
b. Descrever suas criações na área da tecnologia.
c. Enaltecer sua contribuição para o mundo digital.
d. Lamentar sua ausência na criação de novas tecnologias.
e. Discutir o impacto de seu trabalho para a geração atual.

Unit 4 — Establishing and Keeping Relationships

1. Read the comic strip below and choose the best answer to the question that follows. *Scanning*

   Extracted from www.arcticcirclecartoons.com/comics/august-26-2013. Accessed on July 2, 2018.

   What message does the comic strip convey?
   a. The key to establishing and keeping true friendship is to monitor your friends' lives all the time.
   b. Friendship is not always about having extensive dialogues, but rather about understanding the needs and interests of each other.
   c. Ironically, eletronic gadgets prevent friends from talking to each other even when they are near each other.
   d. When making new friends, make sure you have a lot in common. You'll be frustrated otherwise.

2. The modal verb *can* is used by one of the characters from the comic strip in activity 1. In that context, the modal verb stands for...
   a. permission.
   b. ability.
   c. prohibition.
   d. suggestion.
   e. offering.

3. Circle the modal verb that completes all the blanks in this comic strip.

   Extracted from https://br.pinterest.com/pin/459859811945777037. Accessed on July 2, 2018.

   a. can
   b. should
   c. can't
   d. shouldn't
   e. may

4. **Read the sentences. Then use the modal verbs in parentheses to reply to the situations presented.**

   a. Suzanne doesn't have a driver's license. (can't)

   _____

   b. Peter is feeling sick. (should)

   _____

   c. Samantha studies English every day. (can)

   _____

   d. It's very cold outside. (shouldn't)

   _____

   e. This shirt is very old. (should)

   _____

5. **Read the excerpt below and do the activities that follow.**

   "On paper, home sharing sounds perfect. It matches young people, like myself, who can't afford London's rocketing rents, with older people who are lonely.

   As I was about to start a full-time master's course, I was only going to be able to work part-time, so renting a normal flat was out of the question. I searched for alternative options from being a property guardian to being an au pair. [...]"

   Extracted from www.theguardian.com/society/2015/mar/03/young-person-live-older-person-cheap-rent-live-in-care. Accessed on July 2, 2018.

   a. Circle the verbs in the simple past.
   b. Answer the question: What is the infinitive form of the verbs you circled in the text?

6. **Write the simple past form of the following verbs.**

   a. buy _____
   b. see _____
   c. eat _____
   d. look _____
   e. live _____
   f. go _____
   g. be _____
   h. cook _____
   i. do _____
   j. make _____
   k. study _____
   l. learn _____

7. **Rewrite these sentences in the simple past. Make all the necessary changes.**

   a. My father often makes furniture using discarded plastic bottles.

   _____

   b. My best friend studies English in Jamaica.

   _____

   c. I don't share an apartment with my classmates.

   _____

   d. My sister works at Google now.

   _____

   e. My brother doesn't live with his girlfriend.

   _____

8. Complete the excerpts below with the phrasal verbs from the box.

> back off   break up   stand by

a. "[...] Sometimes you don't have to question whether you have good reasons to _____ – you just know it's time. But other times you're not so sure. [...]"

Extracted from www.eharmony.com/dating-advice/breaking-up/15-ways-to-know-its-time-to-break-up. Accessed on July 17, 2018.

b. "[...] Friends are supposed to love you no matter what, but what is important is that they also _____ you. [...]"

Extracted from www.theodysseyonline.com/the-importance-of-having-friends-who-stand-up-for-you. Accessed on July 17, 2018.

c. "[...] If you want to _____ in a relationship, then find the things that you love to do and let them distract you. If you are too wound up in a union, it is easy to make it the center point of your life. [...]"

Extracted from www.lovepanky.com/love-couch/better-love/how-to-pull-back-in-a-relationship. Accessed on July 17, 2018.

9. Choose the phrasal verb to substitute for the word(s) in bold in each sentence below. Then rewrite each sentence with the phrasal verb you have chosen.

a. I might be able to help you financially, but don't **depend on** it.
( ) take after   ( ) count on
_____

b. My father is someone I have always **admired**.
( ) looked up to   ( ) took after
_____

c. Can't you just stop **arguing** all the time?
( ) falling out   ( ) putting down
_____

d. I need one more week to **complete** the project.
( ) stand by   ( ) see (something) through
_____

e. Sean is a great friend of mine. He **is always loyal to** me.
( ) always stands by   ( ) always takes after
_____

f. Everyone says I **am a lot like** my dad, we both love soccer and reading novels.
( ) take after   ( ) put down
_____

g. I **stopped** dancing years ago. I wasn't any good at it.
( ) gave up   ( ) gave in
_____

10. Complete the tasks below with your own information.

   a. Write three abilities you have using *can*.

   _____
   _____
   _____

   b. Write three prohibitions in your school using *can't*.

   _____
   _____
   _____

   c. Write three things friends should or shouldn't do.

   _____
   _____
   _____

AN EYE ON ENEM

ENEM 2014 – Prova amarela

Questão 95

The Road Not Taken (by Robert Frost)

Two roads diverged in a wood, and I —
I took the one less traveled by,
And that has made all the difference.

Disponível em: www.poetryfoundation.org. Acesso em: 29 nov. 2011 (fragmento).

Estes são os versos finais do famoso poema *The Road Not Taken*, do poeta americano Robert Frost. Levando-se em consideração que a vida é comumente metaforizada como uma viagem, esses versos indicam que o autor

   a. festeja o fato de ter sido ousado na escolha que fez em sua vida.
   b. lamenta por ter sido um viajante que encontrou muitas bifurcações.
   c. viaja muito pouco e que essa escolha fez toda a diferença em sua vida.
   d. reconhece que as dificuldades em sua vida foram todas superadas.
   e. percorre várias estradas durante as diferentes fases de sua vida.

Unit 5 — Art: The Language of Emotions

1. Read the article below and choose the option that best summarizes the conclusions of the study. *Skimming*

THE UNEXPECTED, CREATIVE BENEFITS OF SHARING YOUR STUDIO

With the rise of trendy co-working spaces like The Wing and WeWork in recent years, the benefits of such environments have come to the fore. While these companies promise opportunities for networking, career advancement, and off-the-charts idea exchange (not to mention stylish digs), compelling research has found that the people frequenting co-working spaces – like freelancers, entrepreneurs, and remote employees – experience enhanced creativity.

But can the same creative benefits be felt when artists share a studio? You might think the answer is yes, but it's not always the case. Shared studios can help **enhance** creativity, but only if the artists are frequently interacting, **swapping** resources, and exchanging feedback.

Dr. Thalia R. Goldstein, assistant professor of applied developmental psychology at George Mason University, has noted that under the right circumstances, the benefits of co-working spaces can also be felt by artists sharing a studio, by virtue of the fact that it fosters collaboration, as well as the "freedom and time to engage with others," she said.

Multiple research findings back up this notion. At the University of Michigan's Stephen M. Ross School of Business, the first phase of an ongoing study on co-working spaces (chaired by Dr. Gretchen Speitzer, Dr. Peter Bacevice, and Lyndon Garrett) found that the freedom to think and create independently, with self-defined opportunities to join in community, led to a **heightened** sense of achievement.

Extracted from www.artsy.net/article/artsy-editorial-unexpected-creative-benefits-sharing-studio. Accessed on July 19, 2018.

a. Although they are usually used as a cost-reducing alternative for companies and small businesses, co-working spaces are not considered a plausible alternative for artists.

b. Company employees who commonly use co-working spaces are looking for opportunities for networking, career advancement, and off-the-charts idea exchange.

c. According to a study conducted by Dr. Goldstein, shared studios are positive only for artists who are looking for collaboration and the freedom to engage with others.

d. The study concludes that, under the right circumstances, the benefits of co-working spaces can also be found with shared studios. They foster collaboration and also provide artists with the freedom and time to engage with each other.

e. According to Dr. Speitzer, Dr. Bacevice, and Garrett, the freedom to think enabled by co-working spaces makes artists more independent.

2. Read the article again and complete the tasks below.

a. Underline the words with prefixes.

b. Find a word that means *not expected, unforeseen*. _____

c. Find a word that means *talking to each other, working together*: _____

3. Match the prefixes on the left with a word on the right to form new words. Use these words to complete the sentences below.

PREFIX	BASE WORD
over-	biography
auto-	finished
im-	react
dis-	possible
self-	agree
un-	esteem

a. You always _____ to criticism, and it's not a good thing about you.

b. *Long Walk to Freedom* is the name of Nelson Mandela's _____.

c. It's _____ to visit the Sistine Chapel and not be mesmerized by its ceiling. It's wonderful!

d. You might _____, but I think *Guernica* is the most striking painting of all times.

e. *The Gran Cavallo* is one of Da Vinci's most famous _____ works.

f. Some artists have very low _____. They think their work is never good.

4. Read the excerpt below and answer the question that follows.

"Having established his genius as a sculptor and painter, Michelangelo **went on** to completely change the Roman skyline with his architectural designs."

Extracted from www.bbc.co.uk/pressoffice/pressreleases/stories/2004/02_february/05/divine_michelangelo_synopses.shtml. Accessed on July 06, 2018.

The phrasal verb *went on* in the excerpt, whose base form is *go on*, stands for:

a. pass
b. do something without planning or preparing
c. attack someone or argue with someone
d. experience a difficult or unpleasant situation
e. continue

5. Read the definitions for some phrasal verbs with *go*. Then complete the sentences using them.

go for
   choose or accept
go up
   increase in price or value
go over
   review or examine
go out
   feel sympathy or pity
go into
   start to do a particular type of job

a. I need to _____ a few documents before I sign the lease on my art gallery.
b. We need to buy our tickets to the concert before prices _____ again.
c. She plans to _____ teaching after college.
d. Since they are saving money, Mary and Pete decided to _____ the cheapest alternative.
e. Our hearts _____ to the people affected by the hurricane.

6. Complete the table below with the missing words.

SINGULAR	PLURAL
painting	_____
_____	sculptures
picture	_____
wife	_____
opportunity	_____
_____	countries
_____	responsibilities
kid	_____
wish	_____
kiss	_____
knife	_____
museum	_____

7. Complete the sentences below with the plural form of the nouns.

a. Picasso is not only famous for his _____ (painting), but he's also famous for many other art _____ (form).

b. The work of Andy Warhol, one of the most well-known _____ (name) from the pop art movement, has been the subject of multiple _____ (study) around the world.

c. Gustav Mahler, an Austro-Bohemian composer, is mostly known for his _____ (symphony) from the late-Romantic period.

d. _____ (family) are more and more attracted by art _____ (exhibit). Engaging art and technology is an effective way _____ (artist) have found to encourage _____ (parent) and _____ (kid) to visit _____ (museum) and art _____ (gallery).

e. Although only active for about 10 _____ (year), Vincent Van Gogh created almost 900 _____ (work of art).

8. Read the sentence below and circle the option that describes the word order.

> This is a beautiful small round old blue French leather bag.

a. opinion – size – shape – age – color – origin – material
b. size – age – opinion – shape – origin – color – material
c. size – shape – age – color – origin – material – opinion
d. opinion – material – shape – age – size – color – origin
e. color – opinion – size – shape – age – origin – material

9. Check (✔) the correct option to complete the sentences.

a. The *Mona Lisa* is _____ by Leonardo da Vinci. You can find it in the Louvre Museum now.
   ( ) a world-famous portrait painting
   ( ) a portrait painting world-famous

b. Vincent Van Gogh is _____. He was born in the 19th century.
   ( ) a European painter Post-Impressionist
   ( ) a European Post-Impressionist painter

c. The Statue of Liberty is _____ situated on Liberty Island in New York City, USA.
   ( ) a famous neoclassical sculpture
   ( ) a neoclassical famous sculpture

d. *Christ the Redeemer* is _____ of Jesus Christ located in Rio de Janeiro.
   ( ) a colossal Art Deco statue
   ( ) an Art Deco colossal statue

e. The Egyptian pyramids are _____ located in Egypt.
   ( ) ancient pyramid-shaped structures
   ( ) ancient structures pyramid-shaped

f. *Starry Night* is a _____ painting by Van Gogh. It was painted in 1889.
   ( ) fascinating, dark-colored
   ( ) dark-colored, fascinating

10. Describe the following using at least three adjectives each.

a. A place you like going to.

b. An item of clothing you like wearing.

c. A monument in your city or country.

d. A book you have read and liked.

AN EYE ON ENEM

ENEM 2017 – Prova Amarela

Questão 01

Israel Travel Guide

Israel has always been a standout destination. From the days of prophets to the modern-day nomad this tiny slice of land on the eastern Mediterranean has long attracted visitors. While some arrive in the 'Holy Land' on a spiritual quest, many others are on cultural tours, beach vacations, and ecotourism trips. Weeding through Israel's convoluted history is both exhilarating and exhausting. There are crumbling temples, ruined cities, abandoned forts, and hundreds of places associated with the Bible. And while a sense of adventure is required, most sites are safe and easily accessible. Most of all, Israel is about its incredibly diverse population. Jews come from all over the world to live here, while about 20% of the population is Muslim. Politics are hard to get away from in Israel as everyone has an opinion on how to move the country forward – with a ready ear you're sure to hear opinions from every side of the political spectrum.

Disponível em: www.worldtravelguide.net. Acesso em: 15 jun. 2012.

Antes de viajar, turistas geralmente buscam informações sobre o local para onde pretendem ir. O trecho do guia de viagens de Israel

a. descreve a história desse local para que turistas valorizem seus costumes milenares.
b. informa hábitos religiosos para auxiliar turistas a entenderem as diferenças culturais.
c. divulga os principais pontos turísticos para ajudar turistas a planejarem sua viagem.
d. recomenda medidas de segurança para alertar turistas sobre possíveis riscos locais.
e. apresenta aspectos gerais da cultura do país para continuar a atrair turistas estrangeiros.

Unit 6   Sport Is No Longer Just Sport

1. Read part of an article and check (✓) the best title.   *Skimming*
   ( ) Skateboarding in Australia
   ( ) Olympic Skateboarding: Tokyo 2020
   ( ) Rio Olympics was different

www.boardworld.com.au/articles/olympic

1. PARK & STREET DISCIPLINES

If you're wondering which disciplines will be represented at Tokyo 2020, wonder no longer. The Olympic competition will be split into two distinct contests. One will cover street skateboarding – think Street League courses; rails, **hubbas**, ledges, stairs. The other will be a park discipline, which will target transition skaters – think Vans Park Series. […]
As expected, the Olympics will feature both male and female skateboarders competing in each discipline. According to the ISF, the total number of competitors is expected to be around 80, with an equal split between genders. That means we can expect roughly 40 men and 40 women to compete at the Games, possibly split between 20 per discipline, although it's possible that some skaters will compete in both park and street. […]

2. ROLLERBLADERS ARE IN CHARGE – SORT OF

Skateboarding will be governed, at least in part, by the Fédération Internationale de Roller Sports (FIRS). The International Skateboarding Federation was able to **strike** a deal with the Olympics to co-govern the sport alongside our rollerblading cousins, forming the Tokyo 2020 Skateboarding Commission, despite the best efforts of FIRS to take full control.

3. EVERYONE WILL WEAR NIKE

This one almost sounds untrue, but it's absolutely confirmed – at least for U.S. athletes. Part of the U.S. Olympic Commission's massive deal with Nike stipulates that all athletes must be dressed head-to-toe in Nike **apparel** and footwear during all official Olympic engagements. This includes press conferences, interviews, official appearances, and medal ceremonies, however it doesn't extend to appearances in the actual competition, as far as we understand. […]

4. **SPONSORS** WILL BE SILENCED

At the Rio 2016 Olympics, the British Olympic Commission outlined a number of sponsor-related rules that athletes had to accept in order to be allowed to compete. The rules outlaw sponsors who aren't partnered with the BOA from congratulating athletes or even wishing them good luck in a public forum during the Olympic Games.
Any skate sponsor (besides Adidas) must pretend that their U.K. rider is not actually at the Olympics, completely ignoring the competition altogether, or said skateboarder will be disallowed from competing. It's unclear whether this extends to other nations, however considering that Adidas has partnered with numerous Olympic Commissions across the world – including Australia for the past 12 years – it seems likely. Welcome to corporate sports.

5. AUSTRALIA IS WAY AHEAD OF THE GAME

While some nations, namely the USA, have **seemingly** made little progress with their Olympic skateboarding program, Australia has **stormed out** of the blocks. The AOC became the first Olympic Commission to publicly support a skateboarder when they granted Shane O'Neill a $20,000 medal incentive bonus almost immediately after the sport was confirmed for Tokyo 2020. Two Australian skateboarders were recently granted full university **scholarships** as a direct result of skateboarding's inclusion in the Games, while the Australian Skateboarding Federation has already partnered with the AIS for several skate-related Olympic workshops across the country. […]

6. THE OLYMPIC COURSE WILL BE OPEN TO THE PUBLIC

Skateboarding will be held at the Aomi Urban Sports Venue in Tokyo, where street and park courses will be purpose-built for the Olympic Games. Amazingly, the IOC has confirmed that the skateparks will be open to the general public to skate during the Olympics, even on the same day they're used for competition. […]

Extracted from www.boardworld.com.au/articles/olympic-skateboarding-6-things-we-know. Accessed on July 30, 2018.

2. Unscramble the words and write questions. Then match the questions with the answers.

a. contests / the Olympic competition / how many / will / distinct / be split into / ?
_____

b. the skateboarding event / take place / 2020 Olympics / will / where / in the / ?
_____

c. country / has stormed out of / in skateboarding / which / the blocks / ?
_____

d. competitors / event / take part in / the / how many / are expected to / ?
_____

e. sponsoring / for / the / will be / competitors / who / the apparel / ?
_____

f. the skateparks / access / the public / will / to / have / ?
_____

( ) Eighty competitors are expected to participate in the skateboarding event, with an equal split between genders.
( ) The Olympic competition will be split into two distinct contests.
( ) Australia has stormed out of the blocks in skateboarding by supporting its players from the beginning.
( ) Yes, the public will be able to access the skateparks after the events have taken place.
( ) Skateboarding will be held at the Aomi Urban Sports venue in Tokyo.
( ) According to sources, Nike will definitely be sponsoring the U.S. team and maybe that of other countries as well.

3. Fill in the blanks with the comparative form of the adjectives in parentheses.

a. That cat is _____ (mean) than my dog.

b. That sports TV show is _____ (strange) than the one we watched last night.

c. Volleyball player Walsh Jennings's hair is _____ (light) than Logan Tom's hair.

d. Carson's television is _____ (big) than mine. Let's all watch the games there.

4. Read the sentences and check (✓) the options that complete them.

a. Samuel is _____ at sports than me.
   ( ) good
   ( ) better
   ( ) best

b. George is _____ than Robert.
   ( ) funnier
   ( ) funniest
   ( ) funny

c. Soccer is _____ than handball.
   ( ) most popular
   ( ) more popular
   ( ) populous

d. I think baseball is _____ than rugby, but I don't like either of them.
   ( ) bad
   ( ) worst
   ( ) worse

e. I think Serena Williams is still the _____ tennis player in the world.
   ( ) good
   ( ) better
   ( ) best

f. Running is one of the _____ Olympic sports.
   ( ) older
   ( ) old
   ( ) oldest

5. Select the underlined word or phrase that needs to be changed to correct the sentence.

1. The oldest of the triplets is the livelier one, perhaps because he intuitively knows that he is the big brother who needs to take care of everyone.
   a. oldest   b. who   c. livelier   d. big

2. Among the major newspapers in Los Angeles, the more popular one is *The Los Angeles Times*, outselling the four other large publications in the area.
   a. major   b. outselling   c. large   d. more

3. While I enjoy both swimming and running, I am fine at swimming, as I naturally have more upper body strength and feel very natural in the water.
   a. very   b. both   c. fine   d. more

4. The environmentalist isn't sure which is worst for the environment between Styrofoam and plastic.
   a. worst   b. and   c. isn't   d. which

6. Complete the sentences by changing the words in parentheses into a noun using suffixes.

a. The _____ (create) of an independent body to monitor violence on television might succeed in putting these concerns to rest.

b. The _____ (involve) of parents in elementary school classrooms has several benefits for the children's education.

c. The first step should be the _____ (identify) of students who cause trouble in the classroom so that appropriate action can be taken.

d. There is of course a striking _____ (similar) between what happens in the workplace and at home.

e. This is such a common _____ (occur) that the authorities need to take immediate action.

7. Read the quotes and complete them with the words from the box.

creation   inspiration   evolution   ability   arguments   humanity

a. "Genius is one percent _____ and ninety-nine percent perspiration." - Thomas Edison

b. "Silence is one of the hardest _____ to refute." – Josh Billings

c. "Nature used human imagination to lift her work of _____ to even higher levels." – Luigi Piradello

d. "For success, attitude is equally as important as _____." – Walter Scott

e. "To deny people their human rights is to challenge their very _____." – Nelson Mandela

f. "_____ is the fundamental idea in all of life science – in all of biology." – Bill Nye

Source: www.brainyquote.com. Accessed on August 24, 2018.

8. Complete the root word with the correct suffix to form an adjective. You can choose from *-ous*, *-able*, *-ful*, *-y*, or *-ly*. Then use the adjectives to fill in the blanks.

- **a.** danger_____
- **b.** fam_____
- **c.** pain_____
- **d.** help_____
- **e.** sun_____
- **f.** wind_____

a. The way to the stadium was slippery and _____ for Edward to drive on a rainy day.

b. I personally know some of the most _____ sports people in my country.

c. It was supposed to be _____ today for the games, but it's raining. I think we need to cancel them.

d. I tried wearing heels for a day, but it was _____. I wonder how women manage to run with heels on.

e. The surfers were really excited about the big waves because it was _____.

f. Anything you can tell us about the winners would be _____.

9. Underline the correct suffixes to complete the words.

a. I am look_____ (ing / ed) for information about previous Olympic games, but there are too many book_____ (s / es) to choose from in the library.

b. The player who substituted for our goalkeeper was young_____ (er / est) than me. In fact, he was the young_____ (er / est) player in the competition.

c. It was really thought_____ (ful / less) of you to get me a ticket for the game, especially as my son had been so care_____ (ful / less) with the tickets we had bought before.

d. Are you look_____ (ing / ed) for yesterday's paper? After I look_____ (ing / ed) at it, I put it in the recycl_____ (ing / ed) can.

AN EYE ON ENEM

ENEM 2016 – Prova Amarela

Questão 94

Orientações à população são encontradas também em sites oficiais. Ao clicar no endereço eletrônico mencionado no cartaz disponível na internet, o leitor tem acesso aos(às)

- **a.** ações do governo local referentes a calamidades.
- **b.** relatos de sobreviventes em tragédias marcantes.
- **c.** tipos de desastres naturais possíveis de acontecer.
- **d.** informações sobre acidentes ocorridos em Connecticut.
- **e.** medidas de emergência a serem tomadas em catástrofes.

Disponível em: www.ct.gov. Acesso em: 30 jul. 2012 (adaptado).

Unit 7 — Globish: Fad or Fact?

1. What do you remember about the meaning of *globish*? Read the text and answer the question: what is the European form of globish? `Using previous knowledge`

_____

_____

---

www.economist.com/europe/2014/05/24/the-globish-speaking-union

Topics ⌄   Current edition ⌄   More ⌄   Subscribe

WHAT language does Europe speak? France has lost its battle for French. Europeans now overwhelmingly opt for English. The Eurovision song contest, won this month by an Austrian cross-dresser, is mostly English-speaking, even if the votes are translated into French. The European Union conducts ever more business in English. Interpreters sometimes feel they are speaking to themselves. Last year, Germany's President, Joachim Gauck, argued for an English-speaking Europe: national languages would be cherished for spirituality and poetry alongside "a workable English for all of life's situations and all age groups".

Some detect a European form of global English (globish): a **patois** with English physiognomy, cross-dressed with continental cadences and syntax, a train of EU institutional jargon and sequins of linguistic false friends (mostly French). In Brussels "to assist" means to be present, not to help; "to control" means to check, rather than to exercise power; "adequate" means appropriate or suitable, rather than (barely) sufficient; and mass nouns are countable, such as advice, informations, and aids. "Anglo-Saxon" is not a historical term referring to Germanic Tribes in Britain, but a political insult followed by "capitalism" or even "press".

Ordinary Europeans got a first taste of Euro-globish in the televised debates among leading **contenders** for the European election on May 22nd–25th. The idea of the main European political groups picking "*Spitzenkandidaten*" to become the president of the European Commission is a novelty (and has created Brussels's first German neologism in years). It is meant to close the democratic deficit, stir excitement, arrest the fall in **turnout** and check the rise of anti-EU parties.

Of the five *Spitzenkandidaten* debating in Brussels on May 15th, Alexis Tsipras, champion of a far-left alliance, insisted on speaking Greek. Jean-Claude Juncker, Luxembourg's standard-bearer for the Christian Democrats, chose French. The three others gamely abided by the request to speak English: two Germans, Martin Schulz and Ska Keller from the Social Democrats and Greens, respectively, and a Belgian, Guy Verhofstadt, for the Liberals.

[…]

Politics is surely best conducted in the vernacular. John Stuart Mill, for one, thought multilingual democracy a nonsense because "the united public opinion, necessary to the working of a representative government, cannot exist." Yet, as Switzerland shows, a country can have more than one vernacular. In theory that might work for Europe. Mr. Schulz and Mr. Juncker got more prime-time attention when they debated separately on French and German TV in the local tongue. However, even the finest polyglot would **struggle** to reach voters in 24 official languages.

Philippe Van Parijs, a professor at Louvain University, argues that European-level democracy does not require a homogenous culture, or ethnos; a common political community, or demos, needs only a lingua franca. Was Nelson Mandela less democratic for speaking English in multi-ethnic and multilingual South Africa? English is **spreading** fast, with more than 40% of young Europeans **claiming** to be able to speak it in some form. The answer to Europe's democratic deficit, says Mr. Van Parijs, is to accelerate the process so that English is not just the language of an elite but also the means for poorer Europeans to be heard. An approximate version of English, with a limited vocabulary of just a few hundred words, would suffice.

Extracted from www.economist.com/europe/2014/05/24/the-globish-speaking-union. Accessed on July 30, 2018.

---

2. Read the article and answer the following questions. `Scanning`

   a. In which region does "adequate" mean "suitable"? What is the most common meaning of "adequate"? _____

   b. Can you guess from the article the meaning of "Spitzenkandidaten"? _____

   c. According to the passage, which country has more than one vernacular? _____

   d. What do you call a person who can speak many languages? _____

3. Read the statements and write true (T) or false (F).

Understanding details

a. (   ) "Anglo-Saxon" is a historical term referring to Germanic tribes in Britain, but in Brussels it is a political insult.

b. (   ) Ordinary Europeans witnessed the first use of Euro-globish in televised debates among leading contenders for the European election on May 22nd–25th.

c. (   ) During the debate in Brussels on May 15th, Jean-Claude, Luxembourg's standard-bearer for the Christian Democrats, spoke in English.

d. (   ) Mr. Schulz and Mr. Juncker got no prime-time attention when they debated separately on French and German TV in the local tongue.

e. (   ) English is not just the language of an elite, but also a way for poorer Europeans to be heard.

4. Unscramble the words to form questions. Answer them with your opinion.

a. meaning / of / is / Globish / the / what / ?
_____

b. language / official / does / one / Europe / have / ?
_____

c. become / did / world's / English / language / the / how / ?
_____

d. prefer / do / Globish / you / in / English / or / speaking / ?
_____

e. English / is / different / Globish / from / ?
_____

5. Write the correct form of the possessives in the blanks.

a. _____ (People) faith in their own capabilities grows when they see their friends having positive experiences with radical change.

b. Did you watch _____ (yesterday) game?

c. Where is the _____ (ladies) showroom?

d. The pudding would not be to _____ (everyone) taste.

e. _____ and _____ (Anna / Elle) mother invited us to her party.

f. These are our _____ (friends) in our garden.

g. I believe _____ (Ross) English dictionary app isn't the best one.

h. My _____ (parents) friend speaks four languages fluently.

6. Rewrite the noun phrases with the appropriate possessive pronouns replacing the underlined words.

a. Alejandro is your cousin, so is he my cousin, too?
_____

b. Whose umbrella is this? Is it your umbrella?
_____

c. Her eyes are blue; our eyes are brown.
_____

d. Is that your bottle? No, it's my bottle.
_____

e. Can you lend her your shoes? Her shoes are missing.
_____

7. Rewrite the sentences using 's or '.

a. David and Lucy are siblings.
_____

b. All the employees have put their cell phones in the locker.
_____

c. Mr. and Mrs. Rodrigues have a son, Miguel.
_____

d. Alice makes delicious salads.
_____

e. Juan was born on April 30th.
_____

f. The party was at the house of Maria, near the beach.
_____

g. My colleagues have a house next door to ours.
_____

h. That notebook belongs to Gloria.
_____

8. Complete the quote with a pronoun. Then check (✓) the correct option.

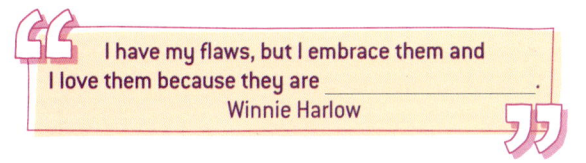

> I have my flaws, but I embrace them and I love them because they are _____.
> Winnie Harlow

Source: www.brainyquote.com. Accessed on August, 9, 2018.

The word you completed it with is a…

(   ) subject pronoun.

(   ) possessive adjective.

(   ) possessive pronoun.

9. Complete the sentences with possessive adjectives and possessive pronouns.

a. Mary has _____ own closet and Mark has _____.

b. She had created this problem and now it was _____ to face alone.

c. Paul and Sabrina's work isn't finished yet, but Lara and Claire finished _____ yesterday.

d. The article on the first page is _____. I wrote it last month.

e. The money is _____, not _____. You and I worked for it, not only me.

10. Identify if the word in bold is a possessive adjective (A) or a possessive pronoun (P).

a. ( ) These are Ana's books. **Mine** are at home.

b. ( ) **Theirs** is the largest English-speaking country.

c. ( ) When you travel, you can take **your** work with you.

d. ( ) **Her** name is fancier than mine.

e. ( ) A friend of **hers** who is a florist asks if she can advertise on the site.

11. Complete the sentences below with the idioms in the box.

> the grass is always greener on the other side
> know your onions
> on cloud nine
> know it by heart
> have a finger in every pie
> a piece of cake
> give it your best shot
> to hit the road
> cold feet
> every nook and cranny

a. They always need to be involved in every project! They _____!

b. I was able to finish the exam quickly because I always read about this topic. I _____.

c. You should study a lot harder to make sure you _____.

d. I looked in _____, but I couldn't find what I was looking for.

e. I know the homework is difficult but _____.

f. Whenever she complains about her town and wants to leave, I remind her that _____.

g. When the bell rang, the teacher told the students _____.

h. Juan was _____ when he discovered that he had been selected to the soccer team.

i. I always get _____ when I have to speak in public, but I guess it is normal to feel nervous before it.

j. This activity is really easy. It's _____!

12. Check (✓) the option with the correct meaning of the idiom / phrase.

a. These two languages have no similarity whatsoever! They are **apples and oranges**.
( ) Both languages are like fruits.
( ) The languages are very different from each other.
( ) The languages have great similarities.

b. José was accusing us of stealing his charger until he found it, and now he's trying **to sweep it under the rug**.
( ) José thinks that his charger will be safer if he hides it under the rug.
( ) José wants to do something to make up for his mistake.
( ) José wants to pretend that the incident never happened.

c. You might think Elizabeth is a kid who has it easy, but if you saw the list of chores her parents give her, I guarantee that you wouldn't want to be **in her shoes**.
( ) You wouldn't want your shoes to get as dirty as Elizabeth's when she's doing her chores.
( ) If you had to do as many chores as Elizabeth, you'd want a pair of comfortable shoes.
( ) Elizabeth has so many chores to do that it is unpleasant to imagine being her.

d. Look at Amanda! She seems to be drawn to painting, just like her father! Well, an **apple doesn't fall far from the tree**.
( ) Amanda looks just like her father.
( ) Amanda's painting and her father's painting look similar.
( ) Amanda's interest in painting is the same as her father's.

e. Anna says she doesn't need any more practice for her piano concert. She **knows the song by heart**.
( ) She knows the song as much as she knows her heart.
( ) She knows the song very well and needs no extra practice.
( ) She sings the song about heart and love.

Unit 7

13. Complete the article with the words from the box.

> common   distinction   work permit   fluent   generation   vocabulary
> fill   eloquence   qualified   oblivious   mile   held

Sir,
As always in his take on Globish, Simon Kuper hits the nail right on the head (FT Magazine, January 13/14).
A _____ must be made between spoken and written Globish. Spoken Globish is fine – we are thankful that there is one _____ language in which conferences can be _____, even if the effortless _____ of speeches or the witty banter during coffee breaks remain the preserve of the Brits.
But written Globish doesn't cut it, ever. A European speaker of English, having learned it as a second language in school, may feel _____ to write entire articles or web texts in the language (ouch). But native English speakers can tell from a _____ away this is Globish, while the person _____ in Globish is _____ to any wrongdoing.
This is good news for subeditors – or (former) translators into English. Obviously, post-Brexit, British subeditors wanting to ply their trade in the EU will need a _____.
So, either the Irish will _____ these posts or Globish might become the new national language of the EU – just until the new _____ that speaks less Globish and more English [...] have brushed up on their idioms (and use them correctly), lost their accent, and expanded their _____.

Extracted from www.economist.com/europe/2014/05/24/the-globish-speaking-union. Accessed on Jul 30, 2018.

AN EYE ON ENEM

ENEM 2016 – Prova azul
Questão 93

Italian university switches to English

By Sean Coughlan, BBC News education correspondent 16 May 2012 Last updated at 09:49 GMT

Milan is crowded with Italian icons, which makes it even more of a cultural earthquake that one of Italy's leading universities—the Politecnico di Milano—is going to switch to the English language. The university has announced that from 2014 most of its degree courses—including all its graduate courses—will be taught and assessed entirely in English rather than Italian.
The waters of globalization are rising around higher education—and the university believes that if it remains Italian-speaking it risks isolation and will be unable to compete as an international institution. "We strongly believe our classes should be international classes—and the only way to have international classes is to use the English language," says the university rector, Giovanni Azzone.

COUGHLAN, S. Disponível em: bbc.co.uk. Acesso em: 31 jul. 2012.

As línguas têm um papel importante na comunicação entre pessoas de diferentes culturas. Diante do movimento de internacionalização no ensino superior, a universidade Politecnico di Milano decidiu

a. elaborar exames em língua inglesa para o ingresso na universidade.
b. ampliar a oferta de vagas na graduação para alunos estrangeiros.
c. investir na divulgação da universidade no mercado internacional.
d. substituir a língua nacional para se inserir no contexto da globalização.
e. estabelecer metas para melhorar a qualidade do ensino de italiano.

Unit 8 — Hit the Road

1. Read the packing list below and answer the question: who is this text for? *Identifying the target audience*

___

Family vacation packing list: the ultimate guide

BY Sally Peck, FAMILY TRAVEL AND BEACHES EDITOR
20 JUNE 2017 • 12:30PM

My grandmother never goes anywhere without a bathing suit and a book – if things are going well, she reasons, she'll get to use both. Make this your policy.

There are, of course, a few other practical things to consider. Check the items below off of your packing list [...].

[...]

For any holiday...

- ( ) 1 **driver's** license, code for rental car; email a copy of both to yourself
- ( ) 2 **tickets** for plane, train or bus
- ( ) 3 **cell phone** and charger
- ( ) 4 **music** on your device of choice for playing in the car (and relevant cable)
- ( ) 5 **wallet** with credit and debit cards and some cash
- ( ) 6 **keys**
- ( ) 7 **camera** and charger
- ( ) 8 **backpack** or another hands-free bag for carrying around daily essentials
- ( ) 9 **clothes**: socks; shoes (at least two pairs); pants; bras; shorts; shirts; warm layers; bathing suit; rainy day gear; pajamas
- ( ) 10 **medication** (anything you regularly take plus Calpol) and a copy of your family's prescriptions
- ( ) 11 **first aid** kit

  [...]

- ( ) 12 **face wash** in a small container, if you're flying
- ( ) 13 **moisturizer**
- ( ) 14 **shampoo** and conditioner for all
- ( ) 15 **toothbrushes** and toothpaste
- ( ) 16 **glasses or contact lenses** plus case and lens solution
- ( ) 17 **sunglasses**
- ( ) 18 **hairbrushes** for young and old, plus hair clips
- ( ) 19 **books** and magazines for all ages
- ( ) 20 **tablet** loaded with programs viewable offline for planes or cars

  [...]

- ( ) 21 **playing** cards
- ( ) 22 **extra bag** for dirty laundry
- ( ) 23 **water bottle** to refill

Adapted from www.telegraph.co.uk/travel/family-holidays/family-holiday-packing-list-the-ultimate-guide/. Accessed on November 12, 2018.

2. Read the text and underline the correct statement(s) about checklists. *Identifying features of the genre*

Checklists...
   a. contain long paragraphs explaining a subject.
   b. contain a set of items rather than long paragraphs.
   c. can be long or short.
   d. are always long.

Unit 8

3. **Read the text again and check (✓) the correct alternative.** *Scanning*
   a. Which of the following categories can you find most in the list?
      ( ) electronics
      ( ) hygiene items and medication
      ( ) food items
   b. Which of the following categories does not appear in the text?
      ( ) food items   ( ) documents   ( ) accessories
   c. Which of the following items from the list could you use on rainy days during your vacation?
      ( ) sunglasses   ( ) playing cards   ( ) bathing suit   ( ) passport
   d. Which of the following items will you need if you get sick?
      ( ) moisturizer
      ( ) a hairbrush
      ( ) medication
   e. Which of the following items are not used for entertainment purposes?
      ( ) books and magazines
      ( ) playing cards
      ( ) a backpack

4. **Complete the sentences with *used to*, *didn't use to*, or *did... use to*.**
   a. _____ be blond! I remember your hair being darker.
   b. _____ she _____ travel by train with you?
   c. They _____ like traveling by plane, but now they do it all the time.
   d. Carla _____ take lots of things in her hand luggage, but now she takes just the essentials.
   e. Joey _____ make a packing list before traveling, but now he always makes one.
   f. Security _____ be so strict in airports. It is much stricter nowadays.
   g. _____ Andy _____ take to the road every weekend before he met you?
   h. I _____ bring any snacks with me on my road trips, but now I always have something to eat.

5. **Underline the correct options to complete the sentences.**
   a. At first I _____ pay attention to the safety instructions at the beginning of a flight, but now I always do.
      a. used to   b. didn't use to   c. didn't used to
   b. He _____ several books a month, but he doesn't have time any more.
      a. used to reading   b. used to read   c. use to read
   c. Did Sarah _____ fasten her seatbelt during takeoff? She didn't fasten it this time.
      a. used to   b. use to   c. used
   d. Caroline _____ the bus, but now she walks to work.
      a. used to take   b. was used to taking   c. is used to take
   e. He _____ a lot of poems when he was younger.
      a. used to wrote   b. used to written   c. used to write
   f. When Pete Smith was the head of our office, everything _____ well organized. Now it's total chaos here.
      a. use to be   b. used to be   c. used to being

133

6. Complete the sentences with *must* or *must not* and the verbs in parentheses.
   a. Passengers _____ (talk) to the driver while the bus is in motion.
   b. I really loved your company. We _____ (meet) more often.
   c. I _____ (finish) this project today. It has to be handed in by tomorrow.
   d. We _____ (miss) the train, because it's the last one.
   e. I _____ (eat) too much or I'll get fat.
   f. He had been working for more than 11 hours. He _____ (be) tired after a long day.

7. Read the article and match the words in bold with their meanings.

> Back when the TSA first introduced its 3-1-1 rules for carry-on liquids, a traveler named Ashley **inadvertently** tried to bring a large, expensive bottle of shampoo through airport security. When the TSA officer threatened to **confiscate** the shampoo, Ashley returned to her airline's counter to check her bag. The line was long, and she was in danger of missing her flight. She **begged** a nearby airline staffer to let her skip to the front of the line; he refused. Only when Ashley started to cry did the **red-faced** airline worker **begrudgingly** allow her to bypass the line.
> She made her flight with minutes to spare – but the airline subsequently lost her checked bag. Says Ashley, "If I had known how much trouble the whole thing would be, I would have just forfeited the shampoo."
> When it comes to packing, a small mistake like putting a **prohibited** item in your carry-on bag can snowball into a messy chain of events. Fortunately, travelers faced with similar packing problems don't have to **rely** on tears to save their vacations. Whether you're dealing with a confiscated item in the security line, a **surplus** of **souvenirs**, a nasty spill, or a broken bag, a bit of packing emergency know-how can mean the difference between a disaster and a worry-free getaway.
> Many travelers forget to save a little extra space in their suitcase for souvenirs. Others only travel with a carry-on, which means that some souvenirs they might purchase, like liquid-filled snow globes, may be prohibited past the airport security checkpoint. […]
> Many travelers ship souvenirs back home – especially large or **fragile** things like handmade Moroccan rugs or Waterford crystal. A **reputable** shop that caters largely to tourists (and sells big and expensive items like furniture) will likely ship your goods back home right from the store. However, without shipping insurance or a tracking number, you have little control over the fate of your purchase.
>
> Extracted from www.smartertravel.com/2017/06/19/5-worst-packing-problems-solve. Accessed on July 31, 2018.

a. _____: say that something is not permitted or allowed
b. _____: trust or depend on someone or something to do what you need or expect them to do
c. _____: respected for being honest or for doing good work
d. _____: officially take private property away from someone, usually as a punishment
e. _____: easily broken or damaged
f. _____: an amount of something that is more than what is needed or used; excess
g. _____: objects that you buy or keep to remind yourself of a special occasion or a place you have visited
h. _____: do something reluctantly because you feel angry, envious, or upset
i. _____: accidently, without realizing what you are doing
j. _____: asked for something in an anxious or urgent way, because you wanted it very much

8. Check (✓) the correct options.

a. What do you call the feeling of confusion and tiredness you have after flying a very long distance?

( ) toll ( ) jet lag ( ) turbulence ( ) deck

b. What do you call a large open container pulled by a train and used to carry goods?

( ) gate ( ) rail pass ( ) wagon ( ) cruise

c. What do you call the place at an airport through which people and goods arriving in a country must pass and where any tax owed must be paid?

( ) lifeboat ( ) customs ( ) rail pass ( ) gate

d. What do you call a vacation on a large ship?

( ) cruise ( ) toll ( ) lifeboat ( ) boat

e. What do you call the irregular and violent movements of air or water that are caused by the wind?

( ) toll ( ) lifeboat ( ) turbulence ( ) deck

AN EYE ON ENEM

ENEM 2013 - Prova Cinza

Questão 95

Do one thing for diversity and inclusion

The United Nations Alliance of Civilizations (UNAOC) is launching a campaign aimed at engaging people around the world to Do One Thing to support Cultural Diversity and Inclusion. Every one of us can do ONE thing for diversity and inclusion; even one very little thing can become a global action if we all take part in it.

Simple things YOU can do to celebrate the World Day for Cultural Diversity for Dialogue and Development on May 21.

1. Visit an art exhibit or a museum dedicated to other cultures.
2. Read about the great thinkers of other cultures.
3. Visit a place of worship other than yours and participate in the celebration.
4. Spread your own culture around the world and learn about other cultures.
5. Explore music of a different culture.

There are thousands of things that you can do, are you taking part in it?

UNITED NATIONS ALLIANCE OF CIVILIZATIONS. Disponível em: www.unaoc.org. Acesso em: 16 fev. 2013 (adaptado).

Internautas costumam manifestar suas opiniões sobre artigos on-line por meio da postagem de comentários. O comentário que exemplifica o engajamento proposto na quarta dica da campanha apresentada no texto é:

a. "Lá na minha escola, aprendi a jogar capoeira para uma apresentação no Dia da Consciência Negra."

b. "Outro dia assisti na TV uma reportagem sobre respeito à diversidade. Gente de todos os tipos, várias tribos. Curti bastante."

c. "Eu me inscrevi no Programa Jovens Embaixadores para mostrar o que tem de bom em meu país e conhecer outras formas de ser."

d. "Curto muito bater papo na internet. Meus amigos estrangeiros me ajudam a aperfeiçoar minha proficiência em língua estrangeira."

e. "Pesquisei em sites de culinária e preparei uma festa árabe para uns amigos da escola. Eles adoraram, principalmente, os doces!"

AUDIO SCRIPTS

Unit 1
Track 02 – Activity 3

a. "We are able to move to these foreign countries where we don't know the language, we don't know the lifestyle, and adapt fairly quickly."

Extracted from https://edition.cnn.com/videos/us/2018/01/12/ Accessed on March 7, 2018.

b. "When Mexico sends its people, they're not sending the best. They're sending people that have lots of problems and they're bringing those problems."

Extracted from www.cbsnews.com/pictures/wild-donald-trump-quotes/9. Accessed on May 6, 2018.

c. "I don't feel as though I have to validate my existence as a citizen of the United States or of the world by my accomplishments but all of my accomplishments are driven by my family and where we're from."

Extracted from https://edition.cnn.com/videos/us/2018/01/12/ Accessed on March 7, 2018.

d. "We have learned to love this country, Mr. President. This country does not belong to you only, but it belongs to all of us."

Extracted from https://edition.cnn.com/videos/us/2018/01/12/immigrants-respond-to-president-trump-orig-tc.cnn/video/playlists/trumps-shithole-comment-and-reaction Accessed on March 7, 2018.

e. "Make us feel safe. We need to feel safe in this country. I think there's a great divide between the races"

Extracted from www.usatoday.com/pages/interactives/trump-nation/#/?_k=wi8jwl Accessed on May 7, 2018.

f. "I believe that he will make America great again and that means a return of jobs. So, in that manner maybe I will find employment."

Extracted from www.usatoday.com/pages/interactives/trump-nation/#/?_k=wi8jwl. Accessed on May 7, 2018.

Unit 2
Tracks 03 and 04 – Activities 2 and 3

Join me as I travel the globe in search of nutrition guidelines!

We begin our journey in Antigua & Barbuda! Antigua & Barbuda have opted for a Food Guide Pineapple which divides foods into 7 groups: starchy foods; vegetables; fruits; food from animals; peas, beans & nuts; fats & oils; sugars and sweeteners.

Next stop is Guyana. Why not display dietary guidelines in a way that people can easily identify with such as a Stew Pot!? Include in your stew staples, vegetables, fruits, legumes, food from animals and fats.

Over we go to Germany. Here we find a German Nutrition Circle. The circle is divided into food groups with numbers representing the quantity to consume, 1 being eat most, 6 eat least, and 7 includes water which sits in the middle. An interesting message they promote is, "Do not overcook your meals" and they also note the importance of meal times by including, "Allow plenty of time for eating and enjoy mealtimes".

We now move continents to South Africa. South Africa only shows food groups that should be eaten that are necessary for health and do not include groups that should be limited such as salt and processed foods. They also encourage local and affordable foods.

While we are in Africa we will visit Namibia. The Namibia food guide shows only 4 groups – cereals and cereal products, vegetables and fruits, beans, and fats, oils, and sugar.

Now we make our stopover in Singapore. Singapore uses a My Healthy Plate model and reminds people to "Use My Healthy Plate to achieve a balanced diet that provides all the nutrients you need each day".

Adapted from https://thedietitianspantry.com/2015/04/01/dietary-guidelines-around-the-world/. Accessed on June 29, 2018.

Unit 3
Track 05 – Activity 2

1. "If you follow Facebook, you know that when they decide they want to enter a market, they can absolutely crush a competitor. Last year, they decided to copy Snapchat stories, introduce that feature. And now Snapchat is really struggling."

Extracted from www.npr.org/2018/05/02/607817969/facebook-to-join-the-dating-game-as-privacy-concerns-abound. Accessed on May 14, 2018.

2. "Well, I haven't quit Facebook. But I think a lot about what happens when I open the app – the good and bad about my complicated relationship with Facebook and social media in general."

Extracted from www.npr.org/2018/04/12/601951556/can-social-media-have-a-structure-that-does-more-good-than-harm. Accessed on May 14, 2018.

3. "How do we proceed so that – just like earlier technologies – we no longer have lead in paint. Our cars have seatbelts and emission controls and airbags, right? We need to put the safety and oversight to our digital tools so that they're not a surveillance machine."

Extracted from www.npr.org/2018/04/12/601951556/can-social-media-have-a-structure-that-does-more-good-than-harm. Accessed on May 14, 2018.

4. "A lot of people are feeling guilty that they're using Facebook, and my response is don't. It's a great product in many ways."

Extracted from www.npr.org/2018/04/12/601951556/can-social-media-have-a-structure-that-does-more-good-than-harm. Accessed on May 14, 2018.

5. "For all the talk of innovation, Silicon Valley right now is a very boring place. Everybody's trying to get purchased by Facebook or Google. That is not an innovative landscape.

Extracted from www.npr.org/2018/04/12/601951556/can-social-media-have-a-structure-that-does-more-good-than-harm. Accessed on May 14, 2018.

Unit 4

Track 06 – Activity 3

Don't let the bully control every day. Every day should be your day, every day should be something that you are in control of. Every day, if you feel like you can't leave the house so you feel like you can't go and play football or tennis or cricket or you feel like you can't go around your friend's house or you feel like you can't go to the shop because you're scared and you want to avoid this person like I felt every day, surround yourself with the people that love and care for you, find the courage somewhere, talk to people. That's what I wish I did.

Extracted from www.youtube.com/watch?v=BCABNJKokIU. Accessed on May 20, 2018.

Unit 5

Track 07 – Activity 1

Occasionally I wonder whether I chose the wrong path in life. If I'd put the same amount of work into an office job or a trade instead of sculpting I may have been much better off financially, but probably not spiritually.

I was one of five children of immigrant Irish parents and grew up hand-to-mouth, for my mother died when I was 10 and my father had to bring us up on his clerk's salary. My parents had that immigrant aspiration for us all and insisted we study for the 11-plus. We all got into grammar school where the expectation was that we'd join the professional upper middle class.

I tried accountancy but it nearly killed me with boredom and I dropped out of art college when my father's house was repossessed. I then got into sign-writing for a supermarket and painted about 60 signs a day for £5.50 an hour which was decent money in the 80s.

One night I saw a program on TV about the Sir Henry Doulton Sculpture School in Stoke where students were given funding for fees and living costs. I immediately knew that's where I wanted to go. [...]

Life changed when I was commissioned to sculpt a herd of bronze Jersey cows for the town square in St Helier. The fee was £220,000 for two years' work and that included the cost of the bronze and other expenses, but what was left over enabled me to self-certify for a massive mortgage and buy a £235,000 smallholding on the Scottish coast in 2002.

[...]

You need strong motivation to make a living as an artist, but if I'd stayed with accountancy I wouldn't have met my wife, had my three children, or lived in this glorious place. There's a saying up here, "What is meant for you doesn't pass by you", and for me that has always been true.

Adapted from www.theguardian.com/money/2018/oct/20/its-precarious-being-an-artist-you-have-lean-and-hectic-years. Accessed on December 13, 2018.

Unit 6

Track 08 – Activity 2

Millennial sports fans are bypassing cable television and abandoning traditional sports for online video game tournaments and other "eSports." Both developments spell a potential headache for professional sports teams, leagues, broadcast partners, and other stakeholders.

Sports fandom is marked by a sharp generational divide. [...] Non-millennial sports fans report spending 41 percent of their media time on TV, but only nine percent of it on online TV. Millennial sports fans report spending much less of their media time (33 percent) on TV - but 20 percent of that TV time is online. [...]

Based on a survey of more than 1,500 U.S. sports fans conducted in the third quarter of 2016, the study also shows that millennial sports fans with at least a "little bit" of interest in eSports significantly prefer their favorite eSports to traditional sports - 27 percent for millennials, versus 13 percent for non-millennial sports fans.

These changes are likely to have implications on viewership for professional sports leagues like the NFL, MLB, and NASCAR, and networks like ESPN, Fox Sports, and individual teams.

Extracted from www.prnewswire.com/news-releases/millennials-abandon-sports-on-tv-posing-threat-to-teams-leagues-broadcast-partners-finds-study-from-lek-consulting-300423351.html. Accessed on September 25, 2018.

Unit 7

Track 09 – Activity 2

Will English always be the global language?

Asking about the future of language is... that way madness lies. Who would have predicted, a thousand years ago, that Latin would no longer be used in a thousand years' time by hardly anybody? You know, I mean obviously Latin is still used in certain circumstances, but it would not be the normal education to be fluent in Latin. If you'd said that a thousand years ago people would have said you were mad. So, in a thousand years' time, will English still be a global language? We could all be speaking Martian, by then, if they land, and take over. You know who knows what's going to happen? To ask about the future of languages is to really ask about the future of... society. And futurologists are just as unclear about what will happen eventually as I am about language. Because language, you see, is global for one reason only, and that is the power of the people who speak it. Power always drives language. There is no other reason to speak somebody else's language other than you want to improve your quality of life, or you want to influence them in some way, or whatever it might be. I mean the tradition in English, of course, English became global for a whole variety of reasons. First of all, the power of the British Empire. Later, the power of American imperialism. Later, in the 17th century, the power of the Industrial Revolution, which meant that the language of science and technology became English, predominantly. In the 19th century, the power of money. Money talks. And the two most productive nations of the world were Britain and America, both using English. So, the language of international banking became the pound and the dollar. English, once again. And then, in the 20th century, cultural power, as you all know, because every aspect of culture you've encountered has some sort of history in the English language, like pop songs, for example, international advertising, air traffic control, the development of radio and television, the development of the internet. Internet, 100 percent an English-language medium when it started, but today, only a fraction of the Internet is English. Internet has become multilingual. So what's going to happen next? English will stay a global language as long as certain things happen. First of all, that the nations that are the recognized as the most powerful nations in the world continue to use English, and all the other nations want to be like them, or want to interact with them, or want to sell things to them, and so on. And so, English will stay like that for as long as those nations retain that kind of power. We're talking mainly America here, aren't we, predominantly? On the other hand, it doesn't take a... it isn't rocket science to think of scenarios where, for whatever reason, American power diminishes, the power of some other nations grow...eh... grows, and you get other parts of the world becoming more dominant and, you know, people say, well what about Chinese, for one day, may be. At the moment, there's no sign of China... China wanting Chinese to be a global language because they're all learning English in China, for the most part. But you could imagine a scenario where it was the other way around. You can imagine a scenario in Spanish, Spanish is the fastest-growing language in the world at the moment, population-wise. Because of South America and Central America, and increasingly in North America, Spanish is becoming very widely used. You can imagine a scenario where, one day, we might all end up speaking Spanish. In another scenario, you can imagine one day we might all end up speaking Arabic. For reasons that are perfectly obvious to anybody who looks at the world. So, all of these things could happen. At the moment, there's no sign of a diminution in the prestige of English. The desire to learn English. The figures are going up, and up, and up every year. At the moment, over 2 billion people speak English. There's never been so many people speaking one language before, and there's no sign of any slackening off in that progress. So, the long-term future, no idea. The short-term future, no change.

Extracted from https://www.youtube.com/watch?v=5Kvs8SxN8mc. Accessed on July 13, 2018.

Unit 8

Track 10 – Activity 2

CONAN: This is Talk of the Nation. I'm Neal Conan in Washington. In 1973, Paul Theroux said goodbye to his wife and children in London and set off on a journey that would make his career and change his life. Theroux was a novelist then, out of ideas, and he hoped that a trip across Europe and Asia and back would inspire a new book. Theroux boarded the Golden Arrow, took the ferry to France, transferred to the Orient Express, and rode the rails east to Iran and Afghanistan, India, Burma, Vietnam, China, and Japan, then home again through the length of the Soviet Union. It took him four and a half months, and he then wrote a now classic book, "The Great Railway Bazaar," which many credit as the start of a new kind of travel literature.

More than three decades later, Theroux retraced his steps as much as he could. There are new train routes, different landscapes, new borders, and different political realities, and he chronicles that trip in his new book, "Ghost Train to the Eastern Star." If you'd like to talk with Paul Theroux about his travels, about what's changed, and what hasn't, along the way, our phone number is 800-989-8255. The email address is talk@npr.org, and you can join the conversation on our blog. That's at npr.org/blogofthenation. While you're there, you can go to our blog and read an excerpt from "Ghost Train to the Eastern Star." That's at npr.org/blogofthenation.

Extracted from www.npr.org/templates/story/story.php?storyId=93702596. Accessed on June 10, 2018.

Track 11 – Activity 3

CONAN: And we're having some difficulty with the studio in Massachusetts where Paul Theroux is going to join us, some technical problems. He's there. We'll be ready to go in just a moment. But in the meantime, why don't we read some excerpts from the "Ghost Train to the Eastern Star"? And this is the beginning:

"You think of travelers as bold, but our guilty secret is that travel is one of the laziest ways on Earth of passing the time. Travel is not merely the business of being bone-idle, but also an elaborate bumming evasion allowing us to call attention to ourselves with our conspicuous absence while we intrude upon other people's privacy".

Well, Paul Theroux, the author of "The Great Railway Bazaar" and "Ghost Train to the Eastern Star", is now with us. He's at the studios of WCAI, the Cape and Islands' NPR station in Woods Hole, Massachusetts, and it's nice to have you with us today.

PAUL THEROUX: Hi. Neal, can you hear me?

C: Yes, you're on the air.

P: Ah, fine. (Soundbite of laughter)

C: I'm glad you made it.

P: No, I made it, but I'm using a common or garden-type telephone.

C: Well, we'll try to get the better connection up as soon as we can figure out the technical problems.

P: OK, that's great. I heard your introduction, anyway.

C: Well, many of our listeners will well remember you as a marvelous traveling companion 35 years ago. You described yourself in this book as jolly in those days.

P: I've always been jolly. You know, if you're a traveler, you need to be optimistic and be in a fairly good mood. I have a reputation for being cantankerous and gloomy, but actually, you can't travel in that mood. And I've always been, I think, in a good mood, thinking there's going to be something good around the corner, even if the corner happens to be Gori in western Georgia.

Extracted from www.npr.org/templates/story/story.php?storyId=93702596. Accessed on June 10, 2018.

Track 12 – Activity 4

C: You rode the Orient Express, but we should be clear, the Orient Express you took was the local, not the luxury, train. In fact, you write that luxury is the enemy of observation.

P: It is. Luxury is the enemy. With luxury, all you say is, I had a nice time. And I don't want to say I had an awful time, but I'd like to, you know, see something, do something. I took the train from Thailand, from Bangkok to the border, Aranyaprathet, but I took a bus because there was no train to Siem Reap. And when I got off the bus in Siem Reap to go to Angkor, I had the option of, you know, lots of hotels but — Siem Reap is a city now of a million people. So, they have five-star hotels and four-star hotels. They have casinos. They have girly shows. They have really everything you want if you're stupid.

But I stayed in a hotel called the Green Town Guest house for 10 dollars a night. And to do laundry was a dollar for two kilos. And I thought, I could stay here for the next two years, you know, at 10 dollars night. I saw some grizzled old men doing pretty much that, actually long-term residents. So, you don't — it wasn't that I was — I didn't want luxury. I thought, this is really pleasant, staying in a place with a courtyard. Eating noodles and paying 10 bucks a night was really pleasant.

I don't know what my total trip cost but some parts were incredibly expensive. Japan is an expensive country. The Trans-Siberian is expensive. But in general, you can get along quite cheaply if you put your mind to it and you don't mind a few cockroaches.

Extracted from www.npr.org/templates/story/story.php?storyId=93702596. Accessed on June 10, 2018.

NOTES

NOTES

NOTES